James, Evan,
I've been wrong before :
2020
37565030748510

SONOMA COUNTY
LIBRARY

OFFICIAL
DISCARD
wind

P9-CAA-920

I've Been
Wrong Before

ALSO BY EVAN JAMES

Cheer Up, Mr. Widdicombe

I've Been Wrong Before

– Essays –

EVAN JAMES

ATRIA PAPERBACK

New York   London   Toronto   Sydney   New Delhi

ATRIA
PAPERBACK

An Imprint of Simon & Schuster, Inc.
1230 Avenue of the Americas
New York, NY 10020

Copyright © 2020 by Evan James

The excerpt on page 141 is reproduced by permission from Francisco Guevara and the UST Publishing House, "Gameness," The Reddest Herring (Manila: UST Publishing House, 2015), pp. 69–70.

All rights reserved, including the right to reproduce this book or portions thereof in any form whatsoever. For information, address Atria Books Subsidiary Rights Department, 1230 Avenue of the Americas, New York, NY 10020.

First Atria Paperback edition March 2020

ATRIA PAPERBACK and colophon are trademarks of Simon & Schuster, Inc.

For information about special discounts for bulk purchases, please contact Simon & Schuster Special Sales at 1-866-506-1949 or business@simonandschuster.com.

The Simon & Schuster Speakers Bureau can bring authors to your live event. For more information, or to book an event, contact the Simon & Schuster Speakers Bureau at 1-866-248-3049 or visit our website at www.simonspeakers.com.

Manufactured in the United States of America

1   3   5   7   9   10   8   6   4   2

Library of Congress Cataloging-in-Publication Data has been applied for.

ISBN 978-1-5011-9964-6
ISBN 978-1-5011-9965-3 (ebook)

Aloud, I said: "The unforeseen is what is beautiful."

—THOMAS BERNHARD, *GARGOYLES*

Contents

"Lovers' Theme"   1

The Land of Sweets   19

Grotesk   35

A Happy Week   49

Just Like That   57

The Garbage Comes from the Garbage   67

My Life as Lord Byron   75

Like God   87

Tonight the Sea Is *Douce*   105

Seven Sensational Party Spaces   111

No Amusement May Be Made   117

A Stranger in Siem Reap   125

On the Loss of Being Here   131

Ghosts of Boystown   149

Designs   155

The Tingler   161

To the Actor   167

CONTENTS

One Hell of a Homie 171

Natural Lives 185

A Sailor's Tale 197

First Date 205

Persuasion 209

Vanishing Days 227

Acknowledgments 241

"Lovers' Theme"

I'm a cell phone. That's what I told myself as I waited for Anna Conda to welcome me to the stage of The Cinch, a gay bar on Polk Street in San Francisco. My heart beat against a pink cardboard flip phone costume that was made by my close friend Kate. I prepared to turn my face—a mask of thick foundation, painted lips, and arched, drawn-in eyebrows, all framed by a wavy blond wig—upon the crowd. (Through a hole in the giant flip phone's screen, I mean. Flip phone prototype: Motorola Razr. This was 2007.)

I'm a cell phone. As soon as Anna Conda called my name—my then-drag name, Extremity—I'd climb the steps, a giant pink ladyphone in black Payless heels, ready to lip-sync a carefully selected medley of ringtones.

"Please give it up for Extremities!"

Amid whooping, laughter, and applause, I heard Kate's voice call out, "It's *Extremity!*" The stage lights glared down on me; I carried myself with as much stylized feminine dignity as a be-dazzled and spray-painted suit of cardboard allowed. The music came on—a loud, cheap-sounding, ringtone rendition of Britney Spears's ". . . Baby, One More Time," all synthesized bleeps and

1

squawks meant to emulate the human voice. I opened and closed my mouth, calling to mind, I hoped, a ventriloquist's dummy.

"*Meep meep meep meep . . . meep meep meep meep . . .*"

The people who attended drag shows in San Francisco generally ate this kind of thing up—part of the reason Kate and I had wanted to put together the number. To my knowledge, no one at any of the drag nights had yet performed as a cell phone, and this novelty provided motivation enough for me to memorize the sequence of ringtone yaps, to roll on pantyhose and fix false lashes to my real ones. Many, many queens had gone to much, much further lengths for their drag numbers, putting hours into elaborate looks and choreography that graced the stage for three minutes. (I once watched, agog, as five-plus people in courtly eighteenth-century European dress—powdered wigs, panniered dresses, deep décolletage—strutted on a tiny stage at The Stud to "Rock Me, Amadeus," inspired by the Mozart biopic *Amadeus*.) Kate and I more often threw things together for conceptual laughs. But that night, as I stood onstage and the Cinch barflies started to sing along, happily providing the vocals to a ringtone version of TLC's "Waterfalls," life felt, for a fleeting moment, simple, perfect.

Bringing absurdist concepts to life suited me better than trying to adopt a persuasive drag persona. This became apparent to me when, after leaving the stage to nourishing applause, I discarded my costume. Made up, bewigged, and wrapped in a length of plain pink fabric, I saw my editor from the local newsweekly at the bar. I freelanced for her often, and we often ran into one another out on the town (in fact, I'd invited her that evening). It was the first time she'd seen me in drag.

"You killed!" she said, laughing.

"Hey, thanks," I said. "I mean, *thanks, honey.*" *How does a real drag queen act?* I thought. *How should a drag queen be?* Still on a giddy stage high, the absence of a protective cell phone casing also left me exposed. I was a turtle that had been pulled from its shell, pancaked with makeup, and let loose in a crowded gay bar.

"You look beautiful," said my editor. "Oh! You need a drink."

Why did the dissonance throw me? I often waded into the strange waters of my competing social impulses: one, to anxiously compartmentalize people so that I could lead multiple lives; the other, to mix the compartmentalized with anarchic disregard like a child swirling finger paint into a muddy blur. Being thrown usually appealed to me: I wanted to see what happened when the colors kissed and started to bleed into one another. If only one of my siblings had dropped by in that moment, along with the elementary school teacher who had long ago encouraged my artistic leanings, along with the butch, menthol-smoking pool player I was then sleeping with and who remained unknown to all my other anxiously compartmentalized friends!

Needless to say, this kind of thinking compromises any unified or consistent social identity. It can make for a fun party, if you have your vulnerably unmasked, half-drunk-and-torn-between-personae party outfit on. I knew that I could never hack it as a serious drag queen, not when I refused to learn how to do my own makeup. (Kate usually did it for me.) I tucked a strand of synthetic hair behind my ear. I smiled, sipped nerve-soothing scotch—through a straw, so as not to imperil my lipstick—and chatted with my editor.

Soon recollected, I went back to mingling, smoking with the sissies, the beefy bears, the indie queers with their trim little mustaches and their skinny arms sleeved in tattoos. After the banter and laughter and a dozen farewell air kisses, Kate drove me to my apartment off Noe Street. There I washed the makeup from my face with baby oil and watched the whole mess run down the drain while I stood naked in the shower, humming a ringtone. Later still, Kate fell in love with a middle school science teacher; my editor became my friend; the cell phone costume sat gathering dust somewhere, and the order of the songs it once called to mind faded from my memory.

———

A little less than two years earlier, at twenty-three, the idea of becoming a real reporter, an actual *journalist*, took hold of me. I'd managed to support myself by freelancing for a couple of years in Portland, Oregon, churning out arts coverage, business-to-business ad copy, and the occasional informational brochure for a master-planned suburban housing community. (More on this last job later.) On the road to the Bay with my oldest friend, Rachel (a lesbian driving a U-Haul to Berkeley, where we *both* planned to live with her girlfriend in a one-bedroom apartment; no further comment), I penned a lofty, confused review of a book commemorating the fiftieth anniversary of Allen Ginsberg's *Howl*. Even then, writing in my notebook as Rachel drove us down the Pacific Coast Highway, I hated the lofty and confused style I brought to the task. *I'll work through this*, I thought. *I'll work through this lofty and confused style, into something more perfect*. At the very least, I considered, writing inside of a speeding U-Haul showed commitment to my ambitions. Not even lesbian relocation could stop me from sullying significant poetry with my posturing opinion (to the tune of ten cents per word, I might add).

It took me a few months, but soon I landed two part-time day jobs, plus a freelancing arrangement with one of the local news-weeklies, plus an editorial internship in the San Francisco offices of *The Onion* (with the local edition of their *real news* arts and entertainment division, *The A.V. Club*). I'd see those offices shuttered before long, but in the meantime a marvelous opportunity presented itself: to make zero money while establishing myself as a writer of frivolous local newspaper articles. Doomsday prophecies about the death of print media hung over the city like one of its famous fogs, but my attitude remained one of, "Why worry about what's to be, when I'm reporting on a Honey Baked Ham storefront for our special print-only Christmas pullout now?"

A paid editorial staff of one managed the San Francisco edition of *The A.V. Club*: a harried and genial music writer named Marc. Marc toiled all day in a private office where precarious towers of CD jewel cases and an iMac that looked like a child's toy covered every inch of space on his desk. His voice, pinched with pressure but still enthusiastic, met me from behind this barricade. "Hey! What's up? What's goin' on?" He often kept his eyes on the computer screen as he greeted me, the white light from the word processor reflected in his glasses.

Out on the sales floor, where another intern and I typically found a desk at which to work, a half-dozen gregarious sales reps passed their days in cold calls and follow-ups. I heard them in the former cases repeatedly explain to potential ad clients that *The A.V. Club* was "like *The Daily Show*." Their comparisons then unfurled into an optimistic pitch for this doomed local enterprise. In their slightly stagey voices I heard the need for a drink grow more urgent over the course of the day.

A twenty-one-year-old girl, who I'll call Daisy, held the other intern position when I first started. She showed up late with a consistency otherwise absent from her work life, having usually stayed out all night drinking or snorting bad cocaine off a video artist's skinny jeans at a Crystal Castles show, or whatever it was she felt compelled to report to me.

"Last night, me and this guy I'm kind of seeing experimented with *knife play*," she once said, trying to provoke me while I fact-checked the music calendar. Her short hair and her malnourished figure stayed almost motionless as she boasted of her exploits, an endless game of conversational chicken ruling her body language. *How far*, her whole person seemed to ask, *how far can I push these reports of my own edginess before you disapprove of me?* "We took turns holding a switchblade to each other's throats while we made out. At one point he ran it along my inner thigh—I couldn't believe how hot it was." I laughed, though she saw little humor in this retelling. "I had multiple orgasms," she added gravely.

Daisy's refusal to work amused me, though it came to perturb Marc. And then my amusement turned to wariness when, several weeks in, she took to looking up from her computer and saying, apropos of nothing, "If only I were a handsome, funny gay man like you. Maybe then I could succeed." Her tone fuzzed the line between compliment and sinister threat, as though weighted with the serious consideration of how to become me. Perhaps through a simple ceremony involving knife play, candles, and a lock of my beautiful, beautiful hair.

I didn't have to worry long; Daisy soon disappeared. Her successor, a pretty Texas transplant, rented her own apartment in Lower Pac Heights, flush with the advantages a fortune amassed through her father's having patented and manufactured a unique grapeseed-based skin care formula.

"Grapeseed," I said when I heard this, my voice a reverent whisper.

Though the Texan never vocalized a longing to steal my identity, now and then she did turn to me and utter some urgent, sage piece of skin care advice, an Anti-Aging Oracle at Delphi. "Do *not* exfoliate your face every day—every few days will suffice," she'd say, or "It's best to wash your face at night and moisturize right before you go to sleep."

One day, while I sat wondering whether I exfoliated my face too often in life, Marc emerged from his office and onto the sales floor, slapping his hands against his thighs like a speed-metal drummer. He approached the intern desk. "Hey!" he said to me. "What's goin' on? Do you want to write a feature about this drag queen pageant?"

The assignment: to report on what was then called the Trannyshack Pageant, by then a San Francisco drag institution just over ten years old. I'd spent a Tuesday night or two at The Stud, the bar South of Market where Trannyshack drew a stalwart crowd most weeks. (Trannyshack was renamed "Mother" several years ago.) What I saw there exploded whatever idea I had about what drag was: nobody paid homage to Barbra Streisand or Gloria Gaynor, but plenty of queens whirled, dervish-like, to Siouxsie Sioux, or channeled the expansive sensuality of a Björk tune, or threw raw meat at the audience.

I accepted the assignment.

Then, of course, I took the assignment too far. Mistaking the Trannyshack Pageant for an opportunity to do some rigorous investigative reporting, I turned what Marc imagined as a light local color piece into an all-consuming task. After waking up at dawn to work one of my part-time jobs, by noon I'd be barreling down Polk on my bike, en route to watch old pageant footage with an eminent queen in her rent-controlled Tenderloin apartment. I scheduled phone interviews with pageant judges in other cities. I checked out books and DVDs about drag from the library. Fascination took hold.

This kind of enthusiasm falls short of remarkable in some ways. The reporter's job remains, as ever, *reporting* on things. Something in my eagerness, though, gives me pause now. Excess appeared not in the probing nature of the questions, but in the compulsive amount. Anxious, I ran from one end of the field to the other, waving my tape recorder; beneath each interview question—"How did your involvement with Trannyshack begin?" "How do you make your breasts?"—lurked a ghostly second question: "And where do I fit into all of this?" I carried on, never knowing when to stop, as nothing close to a satisfying answer to this second question ever arrived. Good thing for deadlines; if I trusted the lengths of my curiosity, I might find myself—I soon would anyway—entering terrain where the personal and the journalistic overlapped, kissed, bled into one another, became one. Though I remained unaware of it then, the prospect of writing my way into something until its scenery surrounded me and became the new, known, intense setting of my life fed further fascination. A better sense of where I stood in relationship to reality, of who I was, and of what it meant to be fully alive, must surely await me beyond the next question, and the next.

It was a lot to ask of newsprint, a lot to ask of wigs, makeup, stage magic. *I'm a cell phone.*

After writing about the pageant, I sniffed out more stories on the "drag beat." Behind the curtain of mundane life teemed this alternate universe, peopled by kings and queens and other mad royalty, all intent on transforming themselves, amusing themselves, joining in a dramatic, raunchy, playful, poised, serious catharsis. The drag performer, filmmaker, and "scream queen" Peaches Christ held midnight movie screenings at one of the many independent theaters then threatened with extinction, staging large *Showgirls* stage tributes. Heklina, the hostess of Trannyshack who took her name from the Icelandic volcano Hekla, put on theatrical drag reenactments of *Golden Girls* episodes. At the height of my mania, I attended four-plus drag events every week. Juanita More got me deliriously stoned at The Stud by lighting a gargantuan spliff and hotboxing the packed bar during her Erykah Badu lip sync. Mercy Fuque, in comic, dejected loneliness, ate a pint of ice cream onstage to Blondie's "Sunday Girl." Stoned or sober, I dreamed of writing a takeoff on Vasari's *Lives of the Artists* called *Lives of the Drag Queens*. The list of names alone suggested a dazzling table of contents: Raya Light, Renttecca, Putanesca, Kiddie, Glamamore, Falsetta Knockers, Holy McGrail, Jupiter, Suppositori Spelling, Fauxnique, Precious Moments.

A class of performers called faux queens came into view. Faux queen, by one definition, meant a biological woman who dressed up as a drag queen—a woman performing as a man performing as a woman (or whatever—at times distinct gender identities at any one of these stages melted in the extravagant fires of persona and performance). This idea, not just once but twice removed from conventional reality, pleased me, spurring on my desire to absorb every variety of blended, blurred, gem-bright persona.

Kate, with whom I later worked on our cell phone bit, was the first faux queen I met. Seven years ago or so, Kate and I reunited at a dinner party in San Francisco. By then I hadn't seen a drag performance in at least two years. I was living in the Midwest. Kate still performed often and now worked as a flight attendant as well. The dinner party took place on Potrero Hill in the home of the former newsweekly editor who saw me the night I dressed up as a cell phone. I was visiting San Francisco for just a few days; the thought of leaving again saddened me. Aside from my editor-turned-friend and her husband, I had visited few former nightlife pals; branded by time and distance, my past and my present now fell into separate, compartmentalized realities. My past appeared to me, from the removed and relatively barren hilltop of the present, more fun in every way. The years had seen Kate and I drift apart despite our delightful shared history. And so, shortly after she showed up to the party, I grilled her about her new life as a flight attendant.

"What's it like?" I asked. "How long are your shifts? Where do you fly? When do you sleep? Do passengers behave differently depending on the route? Have you seen anything terrible happen?" I leaned forward on the couch, cradling a glass of wine in my hand, careful not to spill it on my khakis.

Kate took most available opportunities to share a lurid or absurd anecdote, possessed by her own searching curiosity, a curiosity I thought of as somewhat more zany than mine, less preoccupied with things always slipping away. She met my questions with a familiar glee, regaling me with tales of in-flight rudeness, vomit, and excrement. "I heard that one time," she said, "a huge, drunk Samoan guy got on the plane, puked all over himself, the ceiling, his seatmates, and, somehow, the person *behind* him, then immediately passed out for the duration of the flight."

"Oh my God," I said.

"The daytime flight attendants tend to be more Botoxed and made-up," she said. "They want to marry pilots. The overnight ones, like me, are more likely to be strange—pale, vampiric." She went on to tell me about a daytime flight attendant, the paramour of a married pilot, who flaunted tales of a pregnancy test she had taken at the pilot's house and left on top of the garbage. "The pilot called his wife. He told her he had left some rotten meat in the trash and asked if she could take it out."

I brought my hand to my face in horror, covering my open mouth. The anecdote further poisoned my faith in humanity, meanwhile shoring up my awe. Priceless, in other words. But a pang of regret over our lives forking off in these different directions crept in: I wanted her to keep telling stories, to put on Scheherazade drag, to postpone our return to the present, where we crossed paths with waning frequency.

When I first met her Kate was in art school. Her interest in performance had drawn her out to the drag clubs; at the time she hoped to be adopted and mentored by an established faux queen. Her art preoccupations, however, surpassed typical gender-bending, embracing insect behavior, abjection, "femaleness and the body," and so forth. I once helped her revise a personal artist's statement about transmogrification, which included the lines "I am deeply drawn to things that make no logical sense to me" and "I want to find the deepest, dirtiest point within me and expose it." Though she often found classically draggy ways of turning herself into an absurd, inside-out exaggeration of femaleness, she would just as soon perform, under the name Kegel Kater, as a "drag praying mantis" ripping the head off its mate, or as a kind of hooved, half-drag-queen, half-pony creature in a short art film. Her stage name referenced the pelvic floor exercises named after the gynecologist Arnold Kegel; at art school she had somehow combined Kegels exercises and music in a performance project. I assume she got an A.

With Kate's help, I continued to smear the divide between reporting on drag and being in it. My journalistic objectivity came into question the moment I agreed to play her silent lesbian love interest in a mash-up of American singer-songwriter Jill Sobule's 1995 single "I Kissed a Girl" and the then-trending, filthy viral Internet porn phenomenon "Two Girls, One Cup." Kate sampled the latter's delicate piano music ("Lovers' Theme," by Hervé Roy) for an extended, Sobule-sullying, messy scatological stage freak-out involving a tub of soft-serve chocolate ice cream. Later, we performed a duet at Trannyshack, I the queeny Burt Reynolds to her butched-up Dolly Parton, lip-syncing the wrong-gendered parts to "Sneakin' Around" from *The Best Little Whorehouse in Texas.*

"*I like fancy frilly things,*" I mouthed. "*High-heeled shoes and diamond rings . . .*"

When, in the process of attempting to report on a drag queen/photographer's book of high-artifice, Pierre et Gilles–esque shots of local drag personalities, I ended up sleeping with him instead, Kate became my primary confidante.

"You *what?*" she said.

"He says 'dude' a lot," I offered.

And though I refrained from writing about the photography project out of a sense of journalistic ethics, at that point the words "drag-embedded," once used by Marc to describe my self-made reporter's beat, took on new meaning. Entangled and enraptured, I passed evenings drinking coffee with performers at all-night diners or handing dollars to the queens who walked the narrow aisle at Aunt Charlie's in the Tenderloin, audibly rasping their lip syncs below the pulse of the music. ("*Do you be-lieeeve in life after love? I can feeel some-thing in-side my-seeellf . . .*") That or I rolled a joint and rented a stack of films one queer eminence or another said I simply *must* see—*The Women*, *Eyes of Laura Mars*, *Mahogany*. (My own drag name, given to me by Glamamore, was a buried reference to the latter film and a simultaneous read of my status in relation to the community and the nature of my curiosity and actions—at the edge of things, drawn to extremes.) Red-eyed, dizzy, or trembling with caffeinated energy, I stayed up late almost every night, dashing off a few paragraphs for one of the papers before bed.

All of that felt distant the night of the dinner party. I grew more depressed the more I refilled my wineglass, ignoring the flavor of the wine, which had likely been noted and commented upon at some point during that easy, casual, altogether sane gathering; I hastened to numb myself. Hours earlier, my former editor and I had gabbed through the steps of preparing Flemish *carbonnade flamande* together, chopping onions, browning beef, conjuring a state of warm, happy security. What crisis of time awaited me now? What, now that the heady past lived on in words and wisps of memory alone (and maybe a few videos online)?

Kate and I coming up with some stupid number together: some of the most satisfying moments of those earlier years lived there. At our best, giddy collaboration cemented our bond. One night, I visited Kate at her apartment in the Richmond and found her putting on Hillary Clinton drag in a slowly mounting panic. Someone had asked her to do a Hillary number hot on the heels of Obama's primary win, but now none of her ideas satisfied her. None of the songs, none of the lyrics she earlier thought right for the occasion would suffice. A tense silence gripped the apartment. Kate, frustrated, fine-tuned her makeup at her vanity, moving her eyes between a printed-out photo of Hillary and her own face in the mirror.

"I have an idea," I said. "Look up the Carmina Burana on YouTube—the 'O Fortuna' part."

Kate said nothing. She turned to her computer. She found and played a version of "O Fortuna."

"You could use this," I said. The choir chanted the first lines in dramatic, ominous Latin. I didn't know the meaning of the words then:

O Fortuna	*O Fortune*
velut luna	*like the moon*
statu variabilis,	*you are changeable,*
semper crescis	*ever waxing*
aut decrescis;	*and waning;*
vita detestabilis	*hateful life*
nunc obdurat	*first oppresses*
et tunc curat	*and then soothes*
ludo mentis aciem,	*as fancy takes it;*
egestatem,	*poverty*
potestatem	*and power*
dissolvit ut glaciem.	*it melts them like ice*

"During this part you just stand there at the front of the stage," I said, "and keep a frozen smile on your face. You're trying to stay positive, very political—smiling, smiling, playing the good loser."

The choir chanted into the second passage:

Sors immanis	*Fate—monstrous*
et inanis,	*and empty,*
rota tu volubilis,	*you whirling wheel,*
status malus,	*you are malevolent,*
vana salus	*well-being is vain*
semper dissolubilis,	*and always fades to nothing,*
obumbrata	*shadowed*
et velata	*and veiled*
michi quoque niteris;	*you plague me too;*
nunc per ludum	*now through the game*
dorsum nudum	*I bring my bare back*
fero tui sceleris.	*to your villainy.*

"Now during this second part, you're still keeping a brave face, but you're struggling. Your poise cracks. You find it's harder and harder to conceal your anger and disappointment."

From the slight smile on Kate's face, which looked passably like Hillary Clinton's, I could see my idea gaining hold.

As the timpani and the horns came in and the choir rushed back with more violence on the line "*Sors salutis!*" ("*Fate is against me!*"), I ran around the hall, thrashed my arms, threw myself against the wall, and pantomimed crazed despair. The orchestra cymbals crashed, the choir's lament rose to a crescendo. "And *now!*" I cried. "*Now's* the part where you just go fucking nuts, you freak out, you can't contain your fury—the injustice of it all! Your face—terror! You run around the club, grabbing people in the audience, screaming, '*No! No-o-o! It should've been me! It should've been me!*'"

The two of us broke down laughing. I'd fallen onto my knees, arms raised to heaven. I made my way forward with small, pathetic movements over the carpeted floor.

quod per sortem	*since Fate*
sternit fortem,	*strikes down the strong man,*
mecum omnes plangite!	*everyone weep with me!*

"You fall to your knees, defeated," I said. "Like so."

––––––

A fair amount of progress toward achieving what I thought I wanted sat with me the night of the dinner party. In the intervening years between lip-syncing ringtones and cooking *carbonnade flamande* I had amassed a decent number of soft journalism clips. Today I look back on many of them with embarrassment, with a wish to write new things, like this, in order to blur out the old. One day even this, less than perfect, may provoke the same desire, and so on unto the end, when I leave behind a trail of futile attempts as evidence that I lived—in places, among people, all of us through the storm of time. (When I was a boy, my mother discovered me in my room with a pencil and a stack of paper upon many sheets of which she saw many circles in my childish hand. "What are you doing?" she asked me. "I'm trying to draw a perfect circle," I said, apparently in a state of frustration. How could she know she had witnessed me at the birth of a life's task, and that the task would only become more impossible as my materials, from pencil to my life itself and the memory of it, became more ephemeral? With a pencil or a brush I may conceivably draw a perfect circle, as Vasari in his *Lives of the Artists* tells us Giotto did using red paint; with my life itself and the memory of it I may go on trying, though the materials appear to me, relative to graphite or paint, essentially vulnerable, the circles I manage with them forever disintegrating, the task of redrawing absurd and endless.) I'd gone to work, briefly, as a fact-checking editorial fellow at *Mother Jones*, a magazine of serious investigative reporting to which I contributed little seriousness. (I once set up an interview with a young local politician just because I thought he was attractive.) The night of the dinner party saw me mere months away from completing an advanced degree in creative writing, another field in which I failed to muster much in the way of seriousness but which at least looked a little more kindly upon futile attempts.

That's the CV version, anyway. On Potrero Hill, we drained the wine bottles. The casserole soaked in the sink. We slipped the records back into their sleeves. We extinguished our last cigarettes for the night and prepared for imminent departures. "Good-bye," I said to Kate, who stood at the door with her bright blue motorcycle jacket on, smiling, her helmet tucked under the crook of her arm. "It was so good to see you."

Then time left me a man on a couch with too much wine in his veins. The room, warmed by soft, dim lamplight, tilted if I moved too suddenly; if I moved too suddenly, I became a man walking the cabin of a ship in seesaw. In the valleys of the city below me, the ghosts of a newspaper office stirred: Marc with his gleaming glasses, Daisy with her striped shirts and knives, the sales team cold-calling against the inevitable. Elsewhere the Texan moisturized her face before bed, protecting it from the slow ravages of sleep. Trannyshack's twelve-year run at The Stud had ended; new drag clubs sprouted up, new queens lip-syncing new songs. Who stood witness? Who, reckless, shared the photographer's bed, drawn to breathe in the sharp air of the present at the price of stale professionalism? Somebody handsome, I hoped, and sweet—not a writer, who would write about it later, saying, when asked what he was doing, "I'm trying to draw a perfect circle"—lofty, confused. What sweet friendships bloomed? The pool player, a crushed soft pack of menthols in his breast pocket, leaned over his cue, calculating, taking aim.

I wouldn't sleep well that night. Aside from the wine, insomnia visits me often, keeps me up with its endless questions. *Where do I fit into all this?* The need to catch a plane in the morning added to my worry. Thinking of the plane led me to think of Kate. How many planes would fly before we met again—what new stories would we have to give, evidence of lives once entwined inside a circle, now divided in the wide world beyond? This repetitive fortune, it began to provoke my most unphilosophical hatred. *Sors salutis!* Then I recalled, with great amusement and from my sleepless hold on the couch, one of Kate's latest work anecdotes:

The flight in question had already begun. The plane had already sped down the runway, achieved liftoff, and carried through with its ascent. At cruising altitude, a woman sitting in one of the window seats pressed the call button. A flight attendant made his way down the aisle to see what the woman wanted. When he got there, the woman turned to him, confused. She had been staring out the window, fooled by the solid white of the clouds.

"Excuse me," she said. "Are we moving?"

The Land of Sweets

For a couple of years in my mid-twenties, I was the one you called if you wanted to see the San Francisco Ballet perform *The Nutcracker*. *The Nutcracker* was the company's annual cash cow. Indeed, it's the cash cow for ballet companies all over America because of its whimsical and family-friendly nature. (Unlike *The Dying Swan*, a short ballet re-creating the last moments in the life of a swan—a spectacle no family wants to behold during the holidays.) In the phone room at the San Francisco Ballet during *Nutcracker* season, the lines rang all day long. A flashing red light on the telephone let clerks like me know that even after we'd finished soothing the last frantic mother, another frantic mother awaited us.

"What am I going to tell my kids?" one of those mothers once said to me in the tone she probably used when arguing with her husband. She had five kids and would not accept the idea that I could only seat them apart from one another. Given the scant number of remaining tickets, I would have to scatter them around the highest balcony.

"Some people say you can hear the music better there," I said.

She scoffed. "Who wants to hear *The Nutcracker*?" I wish she had then added, "*The Nutcracker* should be seen, not heard," but that was expecting too much. "We've gone to *The Nutcracker* every year," she said. "It's a Christmas tradition. What am I going to tell them? Sorry, kids, no *Nutcracker* this year? No Christmas?"

If only I had one of those signs up in my cubicle that read, "Your Failure to Plan Does Not Constitute an Emergency for Me," or one that read "Stop, Just Stop." If this frantic mother had really been bringing her children to see *The Nutcracker* for years, she would have known by now that after the subscribers had their pick of seats, the public rushed in like crazed ants toward a mountain of sugar. It strained belief that every year more people wanted to see *The Nutcracker* than were actually able to. There were dozens of performances. The War Memorial Opera House had three thousand seats. But one learns patience working any job that depends upon the hysteria of crowds for its existence. This patience stopped me from saying, "Oh, come on, let your kids sit by themselves. Sitting apart from you could be a whole new Christmas tradition."

My coworker David, a large, soft-spoken man with one glittering stud earring, would sometimes intone the ballet's iconic refrain between calls. "*Duhn* duh-duh-duh *duhn* duhn *duhn* duhn *duhhhhh* . . ." We would all moan and writhe in our cubicles. This melody—heard every time we put someone on hold—had become a kind of Pavlovian hell keen. The Devil would undoubtedly hum it while flaying us alive in our eternal damnation.

Aside from David, the phone room could be divided into two groups: the irreverent young and the old-timers. All of us young still had doe-eyed hope to spare—dreams of becoming envied fashion designers, writers, virtuous social workers. I often worked alongside an optimistic young woman named Katrina. Katrina had her sights set on a more specialized career, too, but it was something very practical—nursing, maybe, or accounting. Whatever it was held no candle to her more immediate and urgent desire to visit Disneyland. She adored the songs and characters of Disney, and would, after she found out I was gay, sometimes ask me questions like, "Evan, which Disney princess is your favorite?"

"*You* are, Katrina," I would say. "*You're* my favorite Disney princess."

"Correct answer," she would say, and then we'd laugh and laugh. Until, that is, I recovered myself and said, "Did you know that Walt Disney suffered from debilitating panic attacks?"

"It must have been hard work being Walt Disney," she said. "Stressful."

"He was consumed by fear and anxiety," I said. "A workaholic, obsessively constructing a fantasy world in order to mask his all-consuming dread."

"Poor Walt," said Katrina. Then she began to sing "Part of Your World" from *The Little Mermaid*.

Toward the end of *Nutcracker* season, my job consisted simply of denying my callers anything whatsoever. No empty seats remained. Changing from one performance to another was impossible. And so I would sit during the evening shift in a small room off one of the somber hallways in the opera house—often it was just me and Katrina, who would softly sing songs from *Aladdin* or *The Lion King* between calls—saying, "No," "I'm afraid not," "I'm sorry, but," and, "No."

An unusual moment from my not-inconsiderable time in the service industry. After so many years spent accommodating people, there's something satisfying about being, for a little while at least, unable to help anyone for a living.

————

The patrons of the San Francisco Ballet sometimes called the phone room to have meltdowns or at least emotional outbursts. The old timers handled these with jaded efficiency (one might occasionally mute her phone to say "God, *this* bitch"; Patti, whose poise and speech called to mind a teacher of elocution or etiquette, might mute hers to mask a sigh, which was about as vocally fed up as she got). But to me these calls were like short, sudden nightmares, the kind of thing from which one woke disoriented, heart pounding. Some callers were simply Machiavellian, like the Pacific Heights dowagers who elbowed away one another trying to get the best seats in Dress Circle, the second balcony. My coworker Dax referred to Dress Circle as "the elephant graveyard"; the subscribers who sat there often called to follow up on rumors of illness or death:

"I know Ruth is too unwell to continue attending, because Celia told me at our weekly book club that they were canceling their subscription. What I want to know is: who's going to get those seats?"

What I wanted to know was: what were they reading at their book club? *Atlas Shrugged?*

Every person, with slight variations, wanted seats closer to the center, the aisle, and the front. I would explain that the San Francisco Ballet had a system for determining who received what seats. "They have a system," I would say, disassociating myself from the company. I hoped that no one would ask me to explain the system, which favored subscribers on a combined basis of seniority and donation. Time and money, in other words. If I was feeling especially besieged, I would pretend that the system ran on an algorithm of unfathomable calculus. It became a mathematical wonder of such complexity that not even I could grasp it.

Occasionally I would receive a call from one half of a particular couple in the middle of a nasty divorce. They had purchased a season subscription together when they were married. Neither, it seemed, was willing to part with the subscription in the divorce, so I played the middleman in their crafty machinations.

"What do you mean she moved the dates for *Giselle*?" the angry husband might say. "*I'm* going to *Giselle* with a *friend*. *She* gets to see *Don Quixote*. Fucking *Don Quixote* . . ." Sometimes they would call on the same day, undermining one another, through me, with their changes of schedule. I imagined that they had both started seeing new people and wanted to impress their dates by taking them to see the ballet in an enviably expensive section of the opera house. This circumstance in itself could have made a nice setup for a second-rate comic opera. I wondered if they had children.

Another day, a regular ballet subscriber called me, her voice reasonable and calm—the voice of a reasonable, middle-aged person willing to calmly discuss things that drove other people to fury. She had just seen one of the performances in her season package—something by Mark Morris, maybe *Joyride*—and had called to praise the choreography and the elegant dancers in her calm and reasonable voice, to laud the loveliness of the dancers and their dancing. Before long, however, she subtly changed the subject. This in a way that had just enough of a trace of nonchalant random association that I should have suspected imminent madness. The formerly calm and reasonable woman wanted to discuss with me the prerecorded voice that came on in the War Memorial Opera House before each performance—another calm and reasonable woman's voice—that reminded ballet patrons to turn off their cell phones and to avoid making excess noise during the performance. As she described this other voice, her own speech began to accelerate.

"That woman should also say something about people covering their mouths when they cough," said the woman. Her voice cracked, grew urgent. "I enjoyed last night's performance, except for the man a few rows in front of me who coughed repeatedly and who each time failed to cover his mouth. Is there anyone I can speak to about adding something to the announcement that woman makes? I just wish they would consider adding something about people covering their mouths." She began to weep. "You know, there has been a spike in tuberculosis diagnoses recently and some people in the audience have weakened immune systems."

For most of this call, I remained silent, letting the woman speak to me, through tears, about her fear of contracting tuberculosis during a performance of *Joyride* or *The Nutcracker* or, in the coming year, *Swan Lake*. (What is it with swans? Something about them seems to provoke a kind of romantic madness, a fear of uncontrollable changeability tinged with the threat of death, as with *The Dying Swan*, or the Greek god Zeus, who transformed himself into a swan to rape Leda. Picasso once folded a piece of paper on which he had drawn a swan in ink, and the inverted image appeared scorpion-like, the elegant face of the swan transformed into a scorpion's venomous stinger, or so I read somewhere.) She seemed like she needed someone to talk to, so I chimed in now and then with a sympathetic "Mmm-hmm," or "That's terrible," the latter because most people simply want to *feel felt*, as a book I once read called *Just Listen* would have it. Nobody wants to be told to calm down. Especially not by a telephone clerk.

In any case, this woman didn't need much encouragement to speak her mind—few patrons of the arts did, and in my position as telephone clerk I often found myself sitting and listening as a caller delivered a tirade born of terror or rage or envy. One woman whose complaint I can't even recall once screamed at me over the phone nonstop for nearly ten minutes, steamrolling any attempt I made to reason by simply screaming even more psychotically. My coworkers at the time watched on as I stood and paced my cubicle with a beleaguered look, occasionally shouting "*Ma'am!*" to no avail, as though I was frantically searching for a woman lost in the nightmarish forest of her own fury. "*Ma'am!*" For those people I felt less sympathy. They wore me down, turned the subscriber hotline into a hotline for their rage. They seemed like miserable demons who required only a telephone connection to slowly poison you with their derangement.

But I felt for the woman who feared contracting tuberculosis. She was not rude, just politely unhinged. In fact, she sounded fragile and vulnerable. I could imagine myself in her position; I too feared many things, like deep water, and accidentally ingesting poison, and working at the San Francisco Ballet for the rest of my life. In fact, I wondered whether or not I was inadvertently ingesting poison at least once a week. I could have been as close to the brink of madness as the woman who sat in her seat in Orchestra, her eyes fixed on the man several rows ahead whose every uncovered cough fed her terror until said terror poisoned her capacity to appreciate Mark Morris's *Joyride*. She finally pulled herself together, apologizing for the way she had gone on about the prerecorded voice while firmly reiterating how she wished its speech would be amended. I think I must have said something like, "Makes sense to me," or, "I completely understand," or "*You're* my favorite Disney princess."

It must be said, that while my job at the San Francisco Ballet paid surprisingly well, provided enviable union benefits, and included perks like discounted tickets to the ballet, the opera, and the symphony, it also filled me with terrible status anxiety and fear. Fear that I would, like one of the old-timers (Gene, who hated Stravinsky, and said of his *Firebird* suite, "Garbage!"), look up and find that a decade had passed. Nobody dreams of being an adequately compensated phone clerk of the Theatrical Stage Employees union, not if you're young and live in America. If you're young and you live in America, it's possible that you'll come to believe, despite any other evidence to the contrary, that you're destined for bigger things. A living wage and unionization fall short of the fantasy of being paid generously to do what you most want to do, of being destined for your own unique mode of greatness.

In any case, at that time I often thought of the San Francisco Ballet—not to say my apartment, my clothes, even the occasional person—as something I had to endure on my way to something better. What a terrible way to live; I would fall into miserable funks, impatient with the contrast between my actual circumstances and the vision I had of myself as bound for some vague creative glory: writer of . . . something that would really amaze people? Glamorous editor of a magazine devoted to . . . beautiful, glamorous things? Public intellectual well-versed in . . . some kind of controversial and interesting topic?

Not once during those years did I take the opportunity to see *The Nutcracker*. I've still never seen it.

Some mornings, on the way to the ballet, I stepped over a homeless man who slept on the doorstep of my apartment. San Francisco had and still has a considerable homeless population. In those years it reminded one of what already felt like a rapidly growing divide between the rich and the poor. (Around that time I also had a job at a hostel in the Tenderloin. European tourists would walk from there to the Asian Art Museum and back, returning with shocked faces. *What is going on in your city?*) Like a lot of people, I would forget about that by the time I sat down in my cubicle. Like a lot of people, I spent a lot of time thinking about how I could probably solve the riddle of my own psychological and existential wounds, my emotional lacks, by buying better stuff. I had, for instance, started smoking Nat Shermans, which were more expensive than other cigarettes but came in a charming box and looked more elegant. I felt like one of those *New Yorker* writers from the 1930s or '40s when I smoked one on my way to scribble in my notebook at Café Flore in the evening.

My coworker Katrina, meanwhile, wanted to visit Disneyland more than ever. A concrete and achievable goal. S.M.A.R.T., like they say: *Specific, Measurable, Attainable, Relevant, Timely*. Well, maybe it was Timeless. She had developed a close friendship with Patti; the two of them began hatching a plan to visit together. "You *know* I want to get my picture taken with Mickey," Katrina would say.

Then Patti might say, "What fun it will be!"

Imagine planning something simply for pleasure, not for self-improvement or advancement! A trip to an amusement park purely for amusement—now that would have never occurred to me. I was more like Jay Gatsby with his little lists: "Practice elocution, poise, and how to attain it," "Read one improving book or magazine per week," "Be better to parents." (Though this last item would have never appeared on my list, since it concerned someone other than myself.) Katrina and Patti planned a pleasurable trip to Disneyland, setting aside money in a reasonable way. I, ever unsatisfied, applied for other jobs. I fantasized, as many do, that I was only a stroke of luck away from finding work at a glamorous magazine, from becoming part of a glittering, trendsetting world of some kind where gazing upon luxury and feeling one deserved it became one and the same. In other words, a world in which you deserved whatever your little heart desired.

When you wish upon a star / Makes no difference who you are . . .

Before long I had secured a job interview with the publisher of the major design and lifestyle magazine *Wallpaper**, whose intitle asterisk led to the tagline "*The stuff that surrounds you.*" That stuff being Italian leather portfolios to hold architectural blueprints, or English bicycles made from Japanese steel tubing. Or four-hundred-dollar headphones from Paris—on which I would presumably spend my days listening to the screams of the hand-to-mouth hoi polloi as I pulled myself up from their ranks. I had at that time used a credit card to buy a thousand-dollar fitted suit—one significantly beyond my means but which I hoped would serve me well in my joyless commitment to upward mobility, surrounding me with an aura of success. "Always leave the bottom button of your suit unbuttoned," a man in another workplace had once advised me. I remembered this in preparation for my interview, for which I had taken the day off from work at the ballet.

I studied my face in the mirror. On the one hand, shaving seemed imperative—the smooth, glossy pages of *Wallpaper** demanded smoothness. On the other, perhaps an affected nonchalance, the juxtaposition of thousand-dollar suit and five-o'clock shadow, would win me more favor. Considering my uncertainty over this small decision, I began to fear that I didn't understand the brand identity of *Wallpaper** at all, and my pre-interview nervousness became even more dire. The stuff that surrounded me included mostly anxious thoughts and despair. I didn't own a razor, either. One often makes bad decisions while anxious, in a desperate and quixotic effort to stamp out anxiety—a futile effort, since anxiety originates with civilization and the steep psychic price of its advantages, its discontents as Freud would put it, and rarely with the perceived conundrum at hand, such as whether or not to shave before a job interview. How had Walt Disney managed? In keeping with this self-destructive pattern, I decided I would simply stop in at the barber for a quick shave on my way to the *Wallpaper** offices. Popping into the barbershop to pay someone else to shave your face seemed like something that the kind of professional I was destined to become might do regularly, casually, without a second thought.

I have pretty sensitive skin. I often walk away from a shave with terrible razor burn, especially on my neck, which is why I now have a full beard. At that time I still believed, or hoped, that the next shave would be different and that someday my skin would adapt to the demands of the civilized, well-shorn workplace. Some part of me knew that to submit myself to the barber's straight razor meant disaster, an act of rank self-sabotage (perhaps self-protection, if one takes the long view of avoiding the seemingly cutthroat—yet delightful and fun—world of lifestyle magazines). In the moment I ignored that reasonable part of myself. In spite of the barber's careful application of hot washcloths and manly-smelling lather, his sharpening the razor against the strop, his surgically delicate movements of the blade, I felt an unpleasant burning sensation along my neck. It would soon be red and irritated, destroying my future in magazines. I would be surrounded not by stuff, but by failure.

The barber began apologizing before he had even elevated my chair to let me see my own face. "I'm sorry, you have very sensitive skin. You should have told me." He looked horrified. He said he had tried to make me look flawless. Now there was nothing he could do. The other barbers in the barbershop looked over in tense silence as I examined myself in the mirror, maybe wondering if I would yell at the barber or cry. I did look like I had been attacked by a wild bobcat. But I understood that I was what was wrong with the situation—I was not like the harpy who had called the ballet to berate me while I shouted "*Ma'am!*"—and so I simply pulled out my wallet and paid up, assuring him that everything was fine.

Half an hour later I sat across from the bald-headed publisher of *Wallpaper** in my thousand-dollar suit, self-conscious about my red and irritated neck, uncomfortably aware of the publisher's disapproving looks. I felt as though my neck were bleeding. It may very well have been bleeding. I felt as though someone had tried, unsuccessfully, to saw my head off. Meanwhile my own eyes probably flickered with the occasional look of intense envy, for I coveted the man's position. At the same time, the entire situation disgusted me.

The publisher asked a question I had not prepared for. (What question *had* I prepared for?) In my memory he may as well have looked into my eyes and, fuming (I remember him fuming, as though my very presence in his office was cause for fury), asked me, "*Why? Why are you here?*"

"I believe I could be a capable ambassador for the *Wallpaper** brand," I began.

"This is an *Assistant to the Publisher* position," he said, impatient.

"I know, I know," I said. "But . . . I believe . . . the stuff that surrounds you . . ."

———

"You've got to be kidding me," said Katrina. "Disney does not have its own legal system."

We were back in the little room in the War Memorial Opera House. It was one of the quieter evening shifts toward the end of *Nutcracker* season. While I shared not a drop of Katrina's enthusiasm for what I called *the moralistic world of Disney* and had no desire to visit Disneyland—in part because of my joyless commitment to upward mobility—I enjoyed chatting with her. On occasion I even semi-begrudgingly joined in to harmonize with her on "A Whole New World" or "Part of Your World" or some other song about waiting for another world. On this particular shift I'd told her a secondhand story about a young man who, while on one of the boats in Disneyland's "It's a Small World" ride, had decided to smoke a joint. At the very moment his thumb had rolled the spark wheel on his lighter, a burly security guard reached out from the shadows on the periphery of the ride and pulled him from the boat. Apprehended, the man was then tried according to a system of Disneyland-specific laws.

"That can't be true," said Katrina.

"I'm just telling you what I heard," I said. "Someone is always watching you there. They have their own laws." If I could see her now, I would tell her the most recent piece of information I'd gleaned about not Disneyland, but Disneyworld. Also related secondhand, it originated with a Brazilian amateur porn actor who briefly worked at that storied theme park in Florida. According to him, new hiring practices specified that anyone working as a character or mascot at Disneyworld must have an American accent, even if their job required no speaking whatsoever.

During the next year's *Nutcracker* season, after Katrina and Patti had gone to Disneyland and showed us photos of their lawful visit, Katrina began getting sick and missing work all the time. We soon discovered that she was suffering from a very rare ailment that disproportionately afflicts young black women. She was out in the hospital receiving special care or treatment and we all hoped for the best—assumed the best, even.

One day, in the middle of what I remember as one of our busier shifts—the red light would be blinking from morning until night—we heard news that Katrina had died in the hospital. She was in her early twenties, like me. The queue of callers didn't know that; life went on not eventually but immediately, urgently, with the red light blinking to let us know our services were required, that frantic individuals remained eager to purchase *Nutcracker* tickets. Some of my co-workers barely held back their tears as they struggled to complete a transaction, waiting to get off the phone so that they could sob in earnest.

Once it was convenient, I rushed out of the office and down the hall, locking myself in the bathroom. I sat on the cool, tiled floor. I held my face in my hands, pressing my palms to my eyes or rubbing my beard, which had grown back after my *Wallpaper** interview. It seemed especially cruel to me—in my still-subconscious belief that one could become exempted from death by working, by upward mobility, which was a movement up and away from death—that death should come for those who still worked in the San Francisco Ballet phone room. Especially that it should come for those who, in their promising youth, had not had enough time to pull themselves up and out and into the kind of work they thought they really wanted to do. Whatever stuff surrounded a person at the offices of *Wallpaper**, it surely wasn't death.

As I remember it, all the clerks managed to carry on that day, grieving in shifts until business hours were over. Those who could pull themselves together got on the phones with either the hyperalert tone of those who came to life in a crisis or the exhausted one of those overwhelmed by the meaninglessness of changing somebody's tickets from a matinee to an evening show. On my way back in, I overheard somebody, one of the old-timers, express surprise at my conspicuous flight from my post. "I didn't know he knew her that well," they said.

They were right to doubt me. I didn't know her well. Patti, who had plummeted with Katrina down Magic Mountain at Disneyland, who had floated with her on one of the "It's a Small World" boats without even thinking about getting high, knew her infinitely better. She carried on with the most aplomb. I heard her apologize to a caller for the long wait, saying, in a steady voice, "You'll have to excuse us, we're short-staffed at the moment. We've just found out that one of our co-workers has passed away. Yes, yes. We're doing the best we can. Anyway, how can I help you?"

I pulled myself together, prepared to take another call. Though it seemed to me that help was beside the point, and that very few people die where they want to. Instead they die exactly where they are. From there they're pulled into the shadows, apprehended. Only then do they learn that some other set of laws, unnoticed till now, has surrounded them all this time.

Grotesk

Me trying to get from Iowa to Georgia—it wasn't pretty. I'd been invited to spend the fall living and writing in the childhood home of Carson McCullers, which was lucky because I didn't really have a permanent home of my own just then: I'd been bouncing between artists' cities and artists' colonies, staying up all night drinking and talking with artists, and making art that no one would buy. I did have a gray 1989 Volvo with more than three hundred thousand miles on it, to which I already owed miraculously safe passage from San Francisco to Iowa. I took it to the shop for a last-minute checkup, crossed my fingers, and set out for the South.

This was late August, 2012. The Volvo's air-conditioning no longer worked, so I spent most of the first day's drive with all the windows half-lowered, sweating as the grim stretch of Missouri that shoulders I-55 rolled by. Because the stereo in the Volvo no longer worked either, I'd picked up a boom box at a Goodwill before leaving, along with copy of Bram Stoker's *Dracula* on tape. In order to hear the actor Alexander Spencer read *Dracula* over the roar of air coming through my windows, I had to turn the volume up as loud as it would go. If you happened to be standing in front of a Shell station outside St. Louis that day, you may have seen a sweaty thirty-year-old from the West Coast on his way to a dead southern novelist's house (*Now, he looks queer,* you might have thought. *Shall my friends and I beat him to a pulp?*), pulling in to pump some gas while a British voice reading the words of a nineteenth-century Irish writer blasted from a car of Swedish make:

"THE PHANTOM SHAPES, WHICH WERE BECOMING GRADUALLY MATERIALIZED FROM THE MOONBEAMS, WERE THOSE THREE GHOSTLY WOMEN TO WHOM I WAS DOOMED . . ."

I spent that night in Memphis. I slept with a dancer who was in a traveling production of—something. *Cats?* No. Never mind. I woke up early to get a cup of coffee downtown and wound up in a shop full of police officers—eight or nine of them, all milling around with white paper cups in their hands. I approached the counter with some trepidation. "Don't make any trouble now," the barista called. "We've got the whole force in here!"

We laughed, and the whole force laughed with us. *This bodes well,* I thought.

———

Columbus, Georgia, where Carson McCullers spent her childhood, sits just east of the Chattahoochee River. Alabama's on the other side of the river. In the kitchen of the McCullers house, my boom box picked up an Alabama public radio station; after writing all day, and before reading all night, I would listen to the radio and cook in the very room from which warm meals once emerged to feed the girl who grew up to write *The Heart Is a Lonely Hunter.* I still haven't read that book, though I meant to do so the whole time I was in Georgia. I had by then read *The Ballad of the Sad Café*, with its surprise wrestling-match betrayal at the hands of a formerly beloved dwarf, and *Reflections in a Golden Eye*, with its closeted army captain, hysterical army wives, and flaming Filipino houseboy. Protected first editions of these and other McCullers books sat in glass cabinets in the dining room. Promotional stills from film adaptations adorned the walls, such as one of a young Alan Arkin as the deaf-mute John Singer deaf-mutely riding a carousel horse.

A letter came to the house shortly after I arrived, from the mayor of Columbus—Teresa Tomlinson, the city's first female mayor. The letter welcomed me to town, then warned me that the food in Georgia could be a little fattening. The mayor also included a clipping about me from the local paper, the *Ledger-Enquirer*, in which my name appeared correctly in the body of the text, but as "James Evans" in the headline. This put a smile on my face. I'd never been written about in a newspaper before, and somehow the mistake made me happier than I would've been if they'd gotten it right. I can't help but feel that life is more like itself when things are going a little wrong.

Writing aside, the primary gift of a residency is ample time half-free from the expectations of the world. The unexpected gift is that one may start, as a matter of course, to reciprocate the favor, relaxing one's expectations of the world in turn. A name misspelled in the newspaper, a surprise interruption by two aging road trippers curious to see where Carson lived, or a rejection from a prospective literary agent saying that the heightened energy of your novel was *somewhat overwhelming* all become occasions not for annoyance or despair, but amusement, curiosity, cheerful drinking.

This was the frame of mind I soon found myself in, anyway, while tinkering with another draft of my novel *Cheer Up, Mr. Widdicombe*. There are only so many hours in the day I can bear this "working with spiderwebs," as a novelist mentor once described the process to me; after that, I eat, clean, shop, talk. It was in carrying out these tasks that I tasted the magic elixir of life in Columbus. Almost every day I would walk to the closest supermarket, Publix. I'd discover along the way that many pedestrian sidewalks in town end without warning, which left me little choice but to walk in the road. In Publix, mothers would run into one another and, after a dance of decorous small talk, get down to gossiping in heavy Georgia accents:

"Oh, her? She goes to the doctor a lot. Always goin' to the chiropractor."

"Chiropractors! Now there's someone who'll always find somethin' wrong with you."

"And it's usually somethin' pretty creepy, if you ask me."

"It doesn't seem to be of much use, does it?"

"I sure doubt it. Though I did go once myself, when my head was misaligned."

I'd be standing there with a packet of bacon in hand, trying to commit this conversation to memory. By the time I thought I had it, some new and noteworthy thing would happen. In this case, while paying for my groceries, my eyes went wide when the cashier, a middle-aged white woman, said to the tall, graying, light-skinned black man in overalls in line behind me, "Good afternoon, Mr. President."

"You don't know how often I get that," said the man.

"Doesn't he look like the president?" the cashier said to me.

The man who she thought looked like the president was grinning my way. He didn't *not* look like the president, but the extent to which his face resembled that of Barack Obama's was debatable enough to make the situation feel fraught. I was just about to respond with what I thought would be the best possible rejoinder—"Which one?"—when the young black man putting my groceries into plastic bags said to me, "Look like *who*?"

"The president," I said.

The young man laughed and shook his head, retreating back into the world of his well-protected private thoughts. Then the cashier held up a bottle of purple Vitamin Water I was buying. "Do you want this now?" she said. "Or are you going to drink it later, so that you can pour it over ice?"

And so I would walk back to Carson McCullers's childhood home, a translucent green grocery bag hanging from each hand, mentally repeating to myself, "Misaligned head, Mr. President, Vitamin Water over ice . . . misaligned head, Mr. President, Vitamin Water over ice . . ." until I could sit down with my diary and a glass of iced Vitamin Water to record these details. Then *Clarinet Corner* would come on—a weekly public radio broadcast during which a man from Alabama and a visiting musician from Kraków, Poland, would talk excitedly about woodwinds— and I'd think, *But I just finished writing down everything that happened to me* outside *the house.* My keenest despair then was that some dazzling facet of daily life such as this would slip from the grasp of my memory, that life would fast outpace the speed at which I could make note of it.

It's harder to keep your thoughts in a philosophically amused, curious frame of mind when something actually unpleasant happens. As a preventive measure against the insane thinking that can come of too much artistic solitude and isolation, I started jogging around the track at Columbus High School in the mornings. What began as a habit driven by commendable sanity soon became one marked by derailing infatuation—what else is new?—when I found that my jogs overlapped with those of a woman and her extremely handsome personal trainer. Judging from his disinterest in my sideward glances at him and his revealing Spandex, he was probably straight as can be. If I had been a closeted army captain like Penderton in *Reflections in a Golden Eye* I might have murdered him out of frustration when he snuck over to my house to sleep with my wife instead of me. Still, my desire to show this unavailable hunk how fit and well-adjusted I could be by running around the track and doing push-ups and lunges led me to overexert myself, and one evening, back at Carson McCullers's childhood home, I threw my back out.

I lay on the carpeted floor of the basement apartment looking at the desk where I wrote every day. I cursed it for having put me in the humiliating position of being so unfit for exercise that I could cripple myself with my own body weight. "So much for life with the personal trainer," I thought, "though now I could use his expertise more than ever."

Pain has a way of compounding any already present sense of being miserably alone in the world. Now I felt more like a character in a McCullers story every day—a lonely gay crushed between the magic of desire and the hell of unrequited lust, a living, breathing part of the so-called Southern Gothic with its so-called grotesques. (The idea of the grotesque has its roots in High Renaissance Rome. Raphael, interested in ancient Roman ruins, had himself lowered by rope into the "grottoes" beneath the Trajan Baths—rooms, actually, that had been part of the domestic wing in Nero's Golden House. The rooms were painted in a Pompeian style in which, according to the historian Daniel Boorstin, "fantastic forms of people and animals were intermingled with flowers, garlands, and arabesques into a symmetrical design." Raphael imitated this style, which was called *grottesche*— "in the style of the grottoes"—when he painted the Vatican loggias. Boorstin continues: " 'Grotesk,' William Aglionby's English treatise on painting explained in 1686, 'is properly the Painting that is found under the Ground in the Ruines of Rome.' ")

Rehabilitation came slow, aided by lame walks around the neighborhood. Passing one house, I recalled a neighbor with a good sense of humor who had come to the reception held for me at the house a few weeks before. He told me he had accidentally seen one of the previous writers in residence walking around the house in her underwear while he was smoking a cigar on his deck. "Hope you don't make a habit of walking around in a similar state!" he joked. "Or is that just something all writers *do*?" I wanted to say that it kind of was. Then he told me I should get an air horn so that if the house was ever being burglarized I could sound it and he would come over with his shotgun.

During these rehab walks I saw many lawns with one or more Romney/Ryan signs staked into them. The election was coming up. I didn't want Mitt Romney to become president, not at all. I wanted the person who came to mind every time the cashier at Publix laid eyes on an older black man with graying hair to run our country. But I'd heard on the radio, from a voter demographic expert weighing in on the debates, that the most influential factors driving American voting habits remained race, religion, and marital status. So I was nervous, having read several frenzied public accusations that the right had put campaign energy into discouraging people of color from voting in strategic places. Confused and discouraged voters during the presidential election seemed to be a pleasing prospect for some people. It was harder to be amused by the world at election time; I often turned off the TV in Carson McCullers's childhood home, disgusted, in the middle of a debate or news of haywire voting machines or a grotesque campaign pseudo-event.

But I still had the cookbook. See, I'd used my Chattahoochee Valley Libraries card—which I obtained by proudly showing my letter from the mayor to a librarian—to check out several books on southern cooking. If I couldn't lay hands on the hot personal trainer or bring myself to read *The Heart Is a Lonely Hunter*, I could at least leave Georgia having tried to learn how to cook a proper pot of greens. This I intended to do by consulting cookbooks, consulting southerners, and making a total mess of the kitchen in Carson McCullers's childhood home. Soon, however, I discovered that the library's copy of *Craig Claiborne's Southern Cooking* held something even better than recipes: another library patron, I assume a southerner who felt very strongly about the ins and outs of their cuisine, had gone through the book and made many alterations, marginal arguments, and irate sentence-level edits. In one paragraph, for example, the phantom editor had crossed out "roux are" and written in an emphatically underlined *is*. In the margin they'd written:

gravy is
roux is
grits is

SINGULAR
oatmeal is
porridge is
rice is

At the end of the paragraph, a penciled-in asterisk decorated the end of a line reading, "One of the most important ingredients in the preparation of a roux is self-confidence." The asterisk led to a scrawled footnote: the words _patience_ and _practice_ stacked one on top of the other. In the recipe for Goldsboro Potato Salad, the editor had violently crossed out the brand name in a note about most of the barbecue restaurants in North Carolina using Hellmann's mayonnaise.

"_NO!_" read the correction. "_Duke's!_"

I shook my head. Now I was going to have to record this in my diary as well. And I'd have to do it while moving between my desk and the floor, depending on which one had become less painful for my back at any given moment. While on the floor I might think, "The great southern novelist Carson McCullers once walked over this floor."

———

One of the guys from the English department at Columbus State gave me a painkiller on election night. My back was improving, but I took it anyway—there was so much more than just back pain to kill. A small group of Democrats from the university had gathered for what we imagined would be a long and bitter night of voter returns plagued by recounts. Then the results came in swiftly and with minimal drama. Good afternoon, Mr. President.

A couple of weeks later, the director of the McCullers Center held a delightful Thanksgiving dinner at her home. She surprised me by saying that her greens recipe used olive oil instead of ham hocks, smoked turkey legs, or some other meat product. I'd been cooking them with ham hocks, a joint of meat that had never crossed the threshold of my own childhood home, where the freezer was regularly stocked with salmon caught by my grandmother and her husband. I imagined the vigilante cookbook editor interjecting:

~~olive oil~~   *NO! Pig knuckle!*

After the toast, we started in on stuffing, turkey, candied yams, mashed potatoes, gravy, green beans. One of the creative writing professors, who had sold me on *HHhH*, a French novel about the assassination of the Nazi official Reinhard Heydrich (actually, I still haven't read it, and it's been years, though I think about it now and then), told me that two men in a neighboring county had been accused of trying to burn a predominantly black church the night of Obama's reelection. Immediately, in other words—had they been standing by with oil-soaked rags and Bic lighters, watching the returns? Looking around the Thanksgiving table at our gathered group of humanities academics, poets, and emerging writers, I wondered what we would have been moved to burn if Romney had won. A golf course? A pile of the Book of Mormon? No, we wouldn't have burned anything—we would have retreated to our separate corners with our copies of *The Canterbury Tales* or *The Heart Is a Lonely Hunter* and maybe a nice glass of Riesling, or else gone onto our preferred news websites and read postmortem commentary about the election.

Later I read in the *Ledger-Enquirer* that the men, thirty-seven and nineteen, burned the Christian flag and an old Bible inside the sanctuary, and tried to ignite pews and a communion table. The cops hit the teen with possession of synthetic weed, too. The paper got their names right, and they reported that their original bonds were set at around $137,000.

───────

Nearly three months had passed. My time in Georgia was coming to an end. My back had benefited from an intense sports massage at the hands of a burly ex-Army lesbian who operated out of an otherwise abandoned-looking building in one of the complexes in Columbus's commercial sprawl, and who told me that I suffered from "military back." That filled me with pride somehow. Political signage had been pulled up from lawns, discarded along sidewalks, or left exactly where it was, signaling unbroken pride or fresh reproach. My senses of wonder and curiosity revived now that, postelection, I expected and wanted less from the world, slipping swiftly back into relative complacency. I would miss Carson McCullers's childhood home, where I had done a great deal of writing, and pulling things up from the grottoes of my mind in solitude, and had read many books, though not *The Heart Is a Lonely Hunter*.

Before I left, I met with a handful of students from the university in the conference room at the house. They ran a creative writing club and wanted to have a Q&A session with me. They'd advertised the event as "Talking with Evan James," which I liked, as it sounded like an intervention, or like they planned on disciplining or dumping me. *We need to talk*. The students, full of a love of literature, full of questions about books, grad school, how to make characters in fiction, and also, how to make money, delighted me.

I did my best. I tried to drive home the importance of every individual honoring his or her own curiosities and taking that which attracted his or her interest seriously. "We should be like Raphael, lowering himself on ropes down into the 'grottoes' beneath the Trajan Baths," I imagine I would say today. I tried to help them understand that writing might even be worth it, because at its best it rewarded curiosity richly, never mind what it was like at its worst, and to persuade them to drink from the elixir of life. (I didn't actually say "the elixir of life." I tried to suggest they drink from the elixir of life without saying so.)

One student asked me if I felt extra pressure living in Carson McCullers's childhood home—pressure to perform under the spectral watch of a Great Writer. I thought for a moment, then said, "No, not at all." I felt the pressure of being alive, the pressure to make something of my own daily America, which was filled to the brim with burning churches, thrown backs, broken Volvos, personal trainers, misaligned heads, sublimated erotic desires, salmon, Scandinavian crime fiction, students asking me whether I felt the pressure—do you feel the pressure? I felt like I might fail but that if I did—and whether failure or success suited me better—would have little to do with Carson McCullers hanging over me like some phantom editor, pencil in hand, over *Craig Claiborne's Southern Cooking*. If Carson McCullers wanted to put any pressure on me from beyond the grave, I doubt it would be critical pressure meant to shape my prose in the image of her own, or to compare my life trajectory with hers and find it wanting. "I'd written three books by your age!"

No. Like any ghost worth listening to, I might find her quarters, painted as they are with fantastic forms, garlands, and arabesques, fascinating; she might, through them, press an asterisk into my mind as I observed, absorbed, took note. The asterisk would lead to a footnote: the word *patience,* the word *practice,* one and the other, bodies fitted together, lovers kept alive on underground walls.

A Happy Week

From the terrace of a coffee shop on Commercial Street in Provincetown, on a breezy July day in 2014, I watched two burly, bearded, sunburned men in camo-patterned shorts and muscle tees struggle to maneuver a huge baby stroller down a flight of steps. "Be careful," said one. "The wheel's stuck." The kid strapped into this juggernaut of child transport kicked his brown legs in the air, cackling as his adoptive parents lifted the whole thing off the ground. Meanwhile, another hairy, muscle-bound type ambled by, gazing my way. At a table next to me, someone said to a friend, "I love this week—everybody's so happy."

He meant Bear Week, the annual wild rumpus for men who, as the *New York Times* once put it, in a phrase more meaningfully active than perhaps intended, "embrace natural body hair." Though not a bear myself (nor a cub, nor an otter, nor a wolf, chaser, or twink; sloth, maybe—where's *our* week?), the thought of this hirsute collective embrace held a certain steamy appeal. At twenty-nine, I still felt compelled, out of a sense of gay piety, to make these pilgrimages to legendary convocations and megaparties, as though I might by doing so come a little closer to being what the man on the terrace said everybody else was—everybody *so* was. So, I had fled my Brooklyn sublet and jumped on a Boston-bound bus in Chinatown, traveling over land and sea to experience this critical mass of body hair and happiness.

On that first full day in town, I felt tired and feverish. I took in street scenes in a state of mild delirium. An Eastern European man trailed passing women, saying in a bored, almost angry patter, ". . . best cupcakes in Cape Cod *yummy yummy yummy . . .*" A young cub couple had a spat; the offended party, dressed in knee-high red athletic socks and bright red short-shorts, rushed ahead of his *beau*, furious. "You can't stop thirty seconds for me? Well, then, I'm not going to stop for you!" An older woman stared, perplexed, at one of those street performers who remain motionless for long stretches—a waif painted white, in white period dress and a white powdered wig. When the Woman in White changed position, her observer observed, with no trace of surprise, "Oh, I see. She moves."

Yes, I thought. *She moves.*

———

The day before, a dilemma struck: en route to Provincetown, I got a voicemail from the woman who ran the Outermost Hostel, where I had a "reservation." Having left on a whim, I'd settled for a bed at this hostel with the charmingly alienated name, assured that I needed no credit card to book—just show up! "I'm sorry, but I made a mistake," said the voicemail. "There are no vacancies after all."

By now I was used to taking the results of my own half-baked planning in stride. (My five-year plan? Make a three-year plan. My three-year plan: make a one-year plan. My one-year plan: do something about all the mistakes I'd made in the previous year.)

At a coffee shop called Wired Puppy, I called several friends with Provincetown histories. I waited. A poet came through for me with the number of a novelist.

When I called the novelist, he answered, "Is this Evan?"

"Yes," I said.

"You poor fuck," he said. Then he gave me directions to his place.

The novelist welcomed me into his living room with a plate of cold fried chicken and a martini. "Is this heaven?" I asked, then thanked him, moved by his hospitality. We ate and drank, chatting about shared literary loves—Giuseppe di Lampedusa's *The Leopard*, Christina Stead's rancid *The Man Who Loved Children*. I enthused over the writer Julie Hecht. "She writes these brilliant short stories about going into discount drugstores on Nantucket fifteen minutes before they close."

My arrival during Bear Week led us, naturally, to riff on gay life. Though straight, the novelist had now lived in a gay resort town for several years. We touched on the remarkable number of middle-aged gay men in Provincetown who—though I mean no disrespect—dressed like seventeen-year-old lacrosse players hired as part of an Abercrombie & Fitch street team. "There's less of an established social standard for aging for gay people," he ventured. "Also, what do you think of that Lady Gaga slogan, 'Born This Way'? I saw it on a T-shirt today."

"Oh, please," I said, happy to hit on a subject that had driven me to heated argument before. "Where's the evidence? And what does being born have to do with anything, anyway? I've spent my whole life trying to forget that I was ever born at all. I think we can do better. How about . . ." I paused, stumped. "A T-shirt with nothing on it?"

"If I hear the words 'born this way' one more time, I'm going to go berserk," he said. After talking with me awhile longer—about Freud, the death drive, a famous pianist who raised wolves on her farm in Switzerland—he rose from the table. "I'm keeping you."

"Keeping me?" I said. "From what?"

"From cruising or whatever else," he said.

I laughed. He led me downstairs to his writing studio, where he had set up an inflatable mattress. I thanked him again, then prepared for bed, too tired to cruise, to say nothing of doing "whatever else"—which, coming from a novelist, could mean almost anything.

———

Over the next two days I explored the town and observed people. I took a bicycle ride out to Race Point Beach and took a nap on the sand, using my shoes as a pillow. I heard rough-voiced Billy Hough sing Crosby, Stills & Nash covers at "Scream Along with Billy" at the Grotta Bar one night. He banged away at a piano that had a tip jar and a skull on top of it. His bass player, Susan Goldberg, after playing a deep intro line, intoned into the mic, "Oh, my God, I am so stoned." I danced in a mob of sweaty, hairy, shirtless bears at the A-House, or Atlantic House, a bar two centuries old. Old for America, in other words. A couple of casual dalliances rounded out what was already feeling like a pleasing Provincetown escapade.

Not wanting to strain the novelist's hospitality but not yet ready to leave, I called another friend of a friend, an artist named Mark who lived in nearby Truro. I was sitting on an orange plastic bench outside the coffee shop Wired Puppy, writing in my notebook, when he rode up on his bicycle.

"You're sitting on Andrew Sullivan's bench!" he said.

I patted my hand against the seat, thinking of the commentator. "I *would* do that."

Mark had a wiry physique. He wore black-rimmed glasses and a sleeveless black T-shirt with white Japanese characters on it. The two of us strolled, stopping into art galleries. One exhibited paintings by his former landlady, who had died a few weeks earlier. In fact, everywhere we went, Mark knew someone.

As we passed the library, I asked about the huge boat I had seen in the center atrium. "It used to be part of the museum that was there before," he said. "Since it was made by a still-living boatmaker, it would have been disrespectful to remove the boat—they would've had to dismantle it. So they built the library around it."

I put our names on the list with the host at a restaurant while Mark rode his bike to his car to drop off our bags. Alone, I wandered the block, looking in shop windows, noting the great many bear couples that appeared to be as good as married. Was Bear Week a couples' retreat?

When Mark returned, we checked in with the host.

"I was looking for you," she said. "Where'd you go?"

"Sorry," I said. "I got distracted."

"He's a wanderer," said Mark.

"I was born this way," I said.

While I cut into a flank steak and Mark ate fish tacos and duck fat fries, he asked me about my notebook. "Is it a part of a mythmaking process?" "No!" I said, startled by this grand characterization. Then I took a moment to reconsider. "Okay, yes. It is."

"I can't remember who said that the first time we remember

an event, it's a memory, but that the second time it becomes a myth."

"It must have been someone very brilliant."

After dinner, and after hanging out at a driveway party down the road, where I smiled to see Mark making out with a young man half his age, we drove to Truro. Out at the "farm," as he called it, it was wonderfully dark and still. We spent a few minutes standing outside his house, which was cluttered with canvases and art supplies, staring up at the clear, starry sky. Then Mark found some aspirin for me in the kitchen—I had a sore throat—and I retired to the guest room.

———

I was glad I visited Provincetown, even though the trip had been different from what I'd imagined. During my time there, I had felt more like a solitary, shiftless drifter than a jolly woodland creature. Yet another reminder to abandon as many expectations as possible upon arriving in a new place, not to waste time bemoaning the clash of extravagant expectations against reality. There's somehow more life in having expectations overthrown than in having them confirmed. But what did I even think I'd find at Bear Week? I must have thought I'd find something. Otherwise, why go? Why go anywhere?

Keen to get back to New York, I boarded a Lucky Star bus in Boston. Though at first relieved to settle in—next to a handsome, bearish young man, no less, a man with strong, thick legs—it soon became clear that a flock of adolescents on a church trip had filled the other seats. As we pulled out of the station, they started to sing in a round. They passed around bags of candy, shouting, "Starburst! Skittles! Swedish Fish!"

My stomach growled. I cursed their failure to absorb and act upon the teachings of Jesus Christ by not abstaining from the gluttony that candy epitomizes.

A thunderstorm darkened the sky above the highway. Lightning flashed. The driver's cautious response to the downpour, plus traffic, was that it would add three hours to our trip. Meanwhile, one of the church boys pulled a pair of bongos from overhead storage and began slapping out crazed rhythms with great energy, not to say cruelty. The thick-legged young man beside me played a game on his cell phone. The sound of virtual gunfire rattled from his headphones while he cursed under his breath: "Mother*fucker!*"

We stopped at a Burger King. All of the churchgoing sprats crowded the line ahead of me. When it came time to leave, they all hooted and hollered back to the bus, bags of food in hand. Though there was no sign of my purchased milk shake and fries, I feared being left behind. I joined them empty-handed, imagining my number called out to an empty Burger King, my food sitting unclaimed on the counter as we drove away.

The sky had cleared by the time we reached the bridge into the city. One of the church girls said to a friend, "You know what I hate about clouds? They're so gorgeous, but when you take a picture of them, they just come out blurs."

"Motherfucker," muttered my seat mate, eyes fixed on his device.

We're almost home, I thought—a specious attempt to convince the part of myself that knew better. Then another church girl shouted up to her chaperone, "What are you preaching on tomorrow?"

The man turned and shouted back, "Suffering!"

"Okay!" she cried. She repeated the word *suffering* to her friends, relaying that tomorrow's sermon would be on that topic, as though none of them had heard the chaperone shout as much. The bongo boy played on. Familiar buildings loomed ahead. What about today? I wondered. I had been to Provincetown now. I had cavorted with bears. I'd expanded my traveler's consciousness, met some nice people, enjoyed a single instance of casual sex. The landscape had stirred my spirit, revived me somehow. If what I'd been on was a pilgrimage, then that must mean that everything I'd seen there, everything I'd done was a living testament to my faith, my beliefs. *I believe in body hair.* I should stand now, preach to those gathered on the bus about what I'd witnessed, what I knew. *God lives here, too. He smiles upon the hairless and the hirsute. He dwells in the beards of Bear Week, in the shrieks of the cub chiding his lover. In the dry martini, in Andrew Sullivan's bench, in the windswept dunes and the young woman I met on the ferry back who believes she is a mermaid. God is a hairdresser by day, a mermaid by night. He is two muscle-bound men carrying a stroller up the stairs. He was born this way—we all were. Listen to me now: I have seen the truth. You need not wait for tomorrow to know suffering.*

Just Like That

Speaking of summer, I once spent part of the summer when I was nineteen working at a gelato cart on the Harbor Steps in Seattle. I say "part of the summer" because this took place at a time when one of my worst old habits—a tendency to quit things suddenly, silently, and without warning—still played a majorly disruptive role in my life and relationships. Though I've since gotten a hold on this tendency, or so I would like to think, back then I was liable to walk away from a job or even a boyfriend so unceremoniously (after months of silently nursing resentments) as to leave people mystified, angry, and deeply disappointed. Nineteen years old that year, I had gotten the job through a high school friend named Caitlin who today owns a diner with her husband. She worked in the main part of the quasi-European café run jointly by a gaunt, intense former physician and an Australian with a goatee while I manned the accompanying gelato cart that faced out onto the public square. It was my first job in a proper city—I had worked in kitchens and at the RadioShack on Bainbridge Island, my hometown, as well as doing various forms of yardwork and landscaping. It opened up a whole new level of service position mischief for me.

A fine-featured, curly-haired man in his twenties helped to train me during the first week. He wore round, black-framed glasses and band T-shirts and approached his work with a level of bright-eyed cheerfulness that made it seem like it might be performance art. He could swerve from smilingly scooping *straciatella* and *pistaccio* for a customer to recommending with dire earnestness that I add Jean-Paul Sartre's *Nausea* to my summer reading list.

(I still intend to read it—perhaps next summer.)

One day we were standing side by side, looking out on the world, watching people go about their business on the Harbor Steps. A woman paced the perimeter of the square. She appeared to be talking to herself.

"Crazy bitch," said my coworker. I looked at him, surprised. He started laughing. "Look closer," he said. I looked, but since he had called her a *crazy bitch* she now only appeared crazier to me, more potentially volatile. Before, she had seemed harmless to my eye; I hadn't made much of the fact that she was muttering to herself. My coworker shook his head. "She's on her phone."

I hadn't noticed that she was wearing some kind of headset. This was in 2002, when the sight of someone making a personal call as they paced around a public space was still relatively rare. If you didn't know better, you could easily take someone talking on a hands-free headset for a lunatic. Now, of course, you really have to listen to what a person is saying to the empty space in front of them to decide if they've lost their mind.

—————

I discovered some strange things about myself at the gelato cart. One of them was a cast of mind I'm not sure how to describe—

something at the crossroads of business smarts, play, and criminal ingenuity. For instance, once the manager came to trust me with running to the bank to change money for the till in the mornings, I hit upon the idea of changing one twenty-dollar bill into twenty Sacagawea coins every day. Just like making calls in public on your cell phone, these coins were new at the time. In fact, they had been something of a controversy, if I remember correctly—Jefferson dollar coins were no longer being freshly minted, and for those who didn't collect coins they felt like inconvenient novelties rather than money if you ever ended up with one. I remember people wondering if the minting of Sacagawea coins was the beginning of the end for the dollar bill; to certain suspicious types it felt European and so somehow decadent, another glinting, post-9/11 sign of a slide into national weakness and decay. To make matters worse, it had a Native American woman on it. There had been one in the till when I first started working at the cart, and when I gave it out experimentally as change the person immediately threw it into my tip jar with the rest of their coins. I figured that if I started giving more of them away, I would leave the cart with more tips every day.

It worked like a charm. I often used part of this haul to buy fresh flowers at Pike Place Market for my first boyfriend, whose father sometimes worked as an Elvis impersonator. More about him in a minute. Another thing I discovered about myself was that, put in the nerve-racking position of serving the public, I began to speak in a faintly European accent, or at least just a little oddly—as though I was not myself, who had been born in Swedish Hospital one neighborhood over and raised on the island just across the water, but a mysterious stranger from elsewhere, unplaceable. (I wish I could say I've shaken off this tendency, but as

I've started traveling abroad more, I notice myself slipping into a kind of clipped, faux-foreign syntax when speaking English—"It is best to call a taxi for the train station?"—perhaps as a way of soothing my own guilt for being born with the silver spoon of the global lingua franca in my mouth.)

"You'll have what flavor?" I'd say. "And scoops—how many you'd like?"

It didn't take long for someone to comment on this performance. One man, a short, tan guy in his late forties or early fifties who wore expensive-looking clothes and who took a special interest in me, returning several times over as many weeks, asked me, while I scooped chocolate gelato, "Where are you from?"

I dropped the accent. "I'm from here," I said.

He narrowed his eyes. "I thought you might be Italian or something," he said. "You have an accent."

"Oh," I said, laughing casually, "that's just the way I talk. I know, it sounds kind of strange. I grew up in . . . unusual circumstances." That was just a line—my family was unusual in its own way, which I'll touch on later, but not in a way that would have led me to fake a vaguely European accent.

The man smiled, apparently charmed by this self-conscious affectation—or else sensing in it an invitation of sorts—and told me that I was very handsome. "I can't believe you haven't been discovered yet," he said, as though it were only a matter of time before I was chewing up the scenery on the silver screen. He then proceeded to tell me about his villa in Tuscany, which he suggested might be an interesting place for me to visit.

In a Henry James novel, this would be the point at which the young American at the gelato cart, naïve but with a robust and pure soul, changed the course of her life by following her suitor to the Continent only to wind up imprisoned in an airless Roman apartment filled with objets d'art, trapped in a marriage with a bickering, hateful, decadent aesthete. As it happened, I had already enrolled in a drawing and art history program in Florence for the following spring—a student-loan-funded escapade that I'm still, to this day, paying for in more ways than one—and so had already taken shortsighted Europhilic escape into my own hands. And aside from that, I was already half a year into my first relationship, even though my boyfriend had cheated on me months earlier while I was recovering from an adult circumcision (picnic, lightning—just kidding: fraught atmosphere around sexuality in the home, intense denial of the sexual self, terrified response to feeling desire for men, isolation, lightning; subsequent humiliating operation and recovery during which arousal was painful, a temporary, accidental, and thankfully unsuccessful form of aversion therapy). Despite that, I exhibited such a high level of pride about my romance—early on, I had, dizzy with pleasure, excitement, and a deep fear of abandonment, confided to a friend that I suspected I might have a special genius for relationships—that I would never dream of betraying him for a financially solvent older gentleman who wanted to spirit me away to Italy as his kept boy.

Privately, however, I responded with relish to this fantasy. It played nicely with my particular craziness, with longings shaped in part by a fatherless childhood, with a reckless desire for adventure and an aversion to prolonged study or work. Perhaps if that man had been more forcefully insistent, I would have surrendered—Lord knows I was looking for male force back then, something powerful to contend with and define myself against. As it was, I made some other excuse. The truth is that I can't say for sure whether I told him that I had a boy-friend. It might be that I told him and that he considered it no serious impediment; it might be that I kept the facts to myself, which would have been like me. In any case, he told me to think about it.

"You'll see me again," he said.

I smiled and gave him his change, which included a Sacagawea coin.

"What the hell is this?" he said, holding it up, turning it around before his eyes.

"It's a dollar," I said.

He threw it into my tip jar. "Keep it."

———

The Australian guy who managed the café and gelato cart was from Sydney. More than once, he told me that I had to travel there one day, specifically so that I could experience Mardi Gras, their massive gay pride celebration. Mardi Gras came up after he asked me if I had a girlfriend, and I replied, proudly, that *no*, thank you very much, I had a *boyfriend*. Friendly man that he was, he responded by detailing his tolerance and even celebration of homosexuality in enthusiastic descriptions of Mardi Gras: the stupendous floats with nearly naked people hanging off them, the thousands gathered in the streets, the bright colors, the joyous noise, the raucous parties that went on all weekend.

I liked the manager—he was chummy, easygoing, and kept us all on task—but found the presence of the owner, a physician by training who had backed the café as a business investment, unnerving. One day when I was standing behind the cart, he came and looked out at the scene on the Harbor Steps with me, launching into a monologue about our flawed and relative perceptions of other people.

"What do you see?" he began, his laser-focused physician's gaze scanning the steps. "Do you see that woman over there? Now, you might describe that woman as big. Maybe even fat; but what are you saying? Big in relation to what? Fat in relation to whom? What does *fat* even mean? We have to work to break ourselves of this habit of limiting our perceptions of others to categorical and societally contingent definitions."

You're the one who called her fat, I wanted to say. I was studying drawing, which demanded peeling back the layer of symbolic abstraction covering everything around us and attempting to perceive and capture specific, individual detail. It wasn't clear to me what I'd done to deserve this particular advice. If anything, I could have stood to shore up my ability to see things in purely symbolic, functional terms, which would have made it easier to go about my daily business with greater efficiency.

On another day—a slow, hot afternoon—the physician praised me for my proactive approach to selling gelato. I had made a few rounds of the Harbor Steps, shouting out "Gelato! Gelato! Ice-cold gelato!" like a carnival barker, herding a handful of people to the cart. I kept him guessing, though: keen to skip out halfway through another shift some days later—I had been working there for *weeks* already and was running out of quick schemes and tricks to keep myself interested, novelty being more important to me at that point than anything else—I feigned nausea and stomach cramps. "I think I might have food poisoning," I said.

"What have you eaten today?" he said, switching into a diagnostic mode.

I couldn't remember. "Old rice," I said.

The physician nodded, curious but unconvinced. "Well, let's see," he began, and then turned his eyes toward the ceiling, calculating aloud how old rice would have to be in order to become host to poisonous bacteria and how long after consuming it a person like me might start to feel ill. "So, it's not impossible that old rice is the culprit."

Old rice. Jesus. I could commit pretty well to a lie at that age, and so I persisted until, at last, I persuaded him to let me go for the day. That was the beginning of my wriggling out of the job for good. Looking back on myself, I shudder: I see a young man who, I believe, craved a harsher discipline imposed from outside, a young man who, to tell the truth, was testing the physician, acting out a kind of neurotic psychodrama. What that young man may have wanted was for someone—the physician, the Australian, anyone—to look him in the eye and say, "Stop fucking around. You're not sick, you just don't want to work. Listen to me: *you need to work*. And you're not always going to like it. You're not always going to enjoy yourself, or be amused, or feel like what you're doing is interesting or novel or cool. But you need to follow through—you need to stand by your word."

I wonder, too, though, if someone did, and he just didn't, couldn't, wouldn't hear them. Caitlin's father, a writer and a lover of Russian literature, tried to suggest all of this in a gentle way after I quit: he emailed me a photo he had taken of Caitlin standing at the gelato cart, her back turned to the camera. *Caitlin's lonely without you!* he wrote.

I don't remember how I justified quitting, which only makes sense, since I had no legitimate rationale. It was a whim: I didn't want to work through the summer anymore. I didn't "like" it.

I was unhappy—more deeply unhappy than I knew, but that would come later. When I sat down with the physician to tell him I wouldn't be coming into work anymore, effective immediately, I gave no special reason that I can recall.

He gave me a hard look, a look of irritation, disappointment, disbelief. "So—no two weeks' notice, nothing? Just like that?"

I held his stare. "Yeah," I said. "Just like that."

Sitting across a café table from me, the physician shook his head, telling me in no uncertain terms how irresponsible my behavior was, how cowardly and pathetic. It's likely that I listened stony-faced, agreeing with each of his correct judgments in turn—though feeling, of course, that he could see only a fraction of the truth about me. "All I can say is that if this is how lightly you treat your commitments," he concluded, "then good luck accomplishing anything of significance in your life."

I left disappointed. Why could he not see the part of me that longed to be seen, that was broken and wounded and desperate to be recognized, to be firmly guided toward some semblance of repair? And why could I not see myself foisting this outrageous task upon an unsuspecting physician-entrepreneur who had hired me to man a gelato cart for the summer?

It would be years before I started turning to myself for help, and trying, in my clumsy way, to lead myself toward the discipline and the courage I desired. In the meantime, I went striding happily away from employment, feeling free as I walked up the street to buy some flowers for my boyfriend. We had a lovely summer together; I dumped him in the fall, unable, or unwilling, to say exactly why.

The Garbage Comes
from the Garbage

I used to like the hot months in New York. And while East Coast companions would roll their eyes—or simply look at me with that "Really? . . . *Really?*" look—when I told them I was "summering" in the city, for several years before moving here that's exactly what I did. Inevitably too broke or shiftless to commit to a full year of rent but forever prey to the charms of this place, I'd sublet a series of sweltering Brooklyn apartments as a seasonal compromise. This is how, in the final year of my twenties, I ended up in a fifth-floor walk-up full of radical lesbian and feminist art.

The sublet in Williamsburg was a step up from the previous year's place, which had come with typed instructions on how to keep the cat from eating the steel wool a former tenant had used to stuff the cracks between walls and floors. I would miss that building's landlords, who were described in the document as "angry ghosts." They showed up in the middle of the night to tinker with the boiler in the basement, or to feed the feral cats in the alley outside my window. In my new place I could contemplate other things, like the flying cockroaches in the stairwell or the artful reprints of bushy vaginas magnetted to the refrigerator.

It was a fine base camp for my yearly campaign of cosmo-politan dissipation. Unfortunately, new technology threatened to disturb my peace at every turn. This was 2012, the year my idle lifestyle fell prey to a handful of smartphone apps for gay men on the prowl.

"Do you think you could ever really date someone you met through a smartphone app?" I asked my friend Emma. "When-ever someone asked where you met, you would have to say *We met through Scruff*, or *Growlr*—oh, God."

"You don't have to say that," she said. "You just make some-thing up."

"That's true," I said. "But you would *know*."

Committed by now to doing one thing and saying another, I set aside my reservations to meet David, a man my age I had been texting with through Grindr.

When I arrived for our date, he was already sitting at the bar, precious craft cocktail in hand. A black woven fedora, the kind I saw everywhere that summer, covered his head. He also wore a soft-looking pinkish-red collared shirt, and I began our date by resisting the impulse to touch it.

David met my eye only occasionally. Instead he looked at his drink or his smartphone. He asked me what I was doing in Williamsburg. When I told him, he insinuated that my spend-ing most of the day reading Henry James didn't constitute work.

"You think it isn't important for me to read books when I'm trying to learn how to write one?" I argued loudly, embarrassing myself.

"You're at about a nine right now," he said. "Bring it down to a five."

"You think that's a *nine*?" I laughed and went on defending my shiftlessness. I quickly tired of the sound of my own voice, though, and started interrogating him about his more legitimate work life. He had been in marketing for a decade, he said, and now handled campaigns for a number of different spirits.

"Spirits?" I said. "What spirits?"

"Alcoholic spirits," said David. "You see, spirits are all about aspirations."

We began, as we sipped our way through another cocktail each—cocktails made with elderflower liqueur, top-shelf tequilas, I think one of them contained gunpowder—to parse the aspirations associated with different spirits, the ways in which drinkers revealed their fantasies of upward mobility by their brand loyalty.

"Tanqueray is ghetto fabulous," said David. "Grey Goose is pure, clean—the country club. I once had to interview the powerful, gay former editor of a magazine for market research. He said to me, 'Dark liquors make me crazy.' Most of the times *I've* gotten really wild, it's been while I was drinking Jack Daniel's."

"Have some Jack Daniel's," I said.

Everything ever said about alcohol being true, my feelings of resistance to David began to burn up in the heat of an obvious, aggravating mutual attraction. This kept us arguing until three hours had passed and we'd downed six fancy cocktails each.

"Damn, you can really drink," said David.

"I'm Russian, Irish, and Welsh," I said.

Flush with aspirations, awash with romance, our conversation turned to the most romantic subject of all: travel. David had travel plans spanning four years; he wanted to see Australia, Brazil, Hawaii, Tokyo, and Eastern Europe. Privately I thought that these plans must coincide with the aspirations associated with his preferred brands of liquor—but how? In the spirit of wanderlust, one of us suggested leaving the bar for a stroll. David was standing, and when a young woman tried to take the stool he had been sitting on, he stopped her. Once she had walked out of earshot, he looked affronted, and casually called the woman a bitch. An overreaction, I thought. I recalled the décor in my sublet. What would happen if I brought David home with me? All those pictures of vaginas. All those bitches.

"You're at about a nine right now," I said. "Bring it down to a five."

Outside, the night was mild and cool. David suggested we stroll to the Northside Piers. We stopped to kiss along the way, half-joking about what we would do if a pack of homophobes saw us and decided to beat us senseless. "I would run away and call 911 while you fought them," I offered.

"I could see that," he said.

We sat down together on a bench, on a dark stretch of pier, admiring the city lit up across the water. I wrapped my arm around his shoulder. He was asleep, actually *asleep*, within minutes. I took off his fedora and rested my chin on his balding head. In the distance, a train snaked lazily along its track.

David stirred. "Can I say something?" he said. Then he said the something he had asked permission to say: "This feels right."

I rubbed his shoulder, buying myself time. What he'd said was heart-warming. Nevertheless, I decided at that moment that any possibly serious relationship between us was doomed. Almost nothing, aside from perhaps sleep, couch-bound inertia, and sometimes reading, ever felt right to me. Perhaps there are two kinds of people: those for whom things feel right and those for whom they never will. But on a first date you just can't say, "This feels neither right nor wrong." I felt that I would be alone for all my life. Cosmically, fundamentally alone. I rubbed his shoulder again, this time with more affection—the terrified kind.

With our respective feelings of rightness and of cosmic aloneness, we strolled away from the piers, toward Bedford. I would invite David back to my sublet, to spend the night with me and all the radical feminist and lesbian décor. On the way, I stopped outside a large condo, along the side of which stood a wall of bulging garbage bags—more garbage than I had ever seen in one place outside of a landfill. I took his hand in mine, pretending garbage was romantic.

"Where does all this garbage come from?" I said dreamily, staring at the black wall.

David gave me a baffled look. "What do you mean, 'Where does all this garbage come from?' The garbage comes from the garbage. Where the hell do you think it comes from?"

———

Shortly after our first date, David left for a long weekend in Miami. During this time I imagined he was using one of the gay cruising apps, or else his simple and winning feeling of rightness, to lure other men into bed with him. The idea didn't bother me. He knew I would be leaving New York soon, so neither of us seemed to entertain any illusions about the longevity of our relationship (aside, that is, from the illusion of not entertaining any illusions—an illusion that afflicts us all).

In any case, David and I planned to see each other again when he returned. *This time,* I thought, *we'll really and fully consummate our summer fling. We'll go to bed together in a direct and uncomplicated way, the way Grindr intended. Enough of all this excavating, enough of the impossibility of ever fully understanding oneself or anyone else. As the 1960 George Cukor film starring Marilyn Monroe would have it,* Let's Make Love!

Within twenty-four hours of having this thought, I began to feel more lethargic than usual. I beat a hasty retreat to my sublet, where I shivered and sweated, hit by some heavy summer bug. I downed a capful of generic-brand, semihallucinogenic orange syrup. What aspirations did *this* spirit reveal?

I sent David a text message to let him know I wasn't feeling well, and that we should probably call off our date.

"Need anything?" David wrote back. "Soup? Drugs?"

Yes, I wrote, I would like soup and drugs.

When he arrived hours later, he found me staring at a pyramidal shelf in the corner that supported a garden of potted succulents. In one hand he held a white plastic shopping bag containing the soup and more cold syrup; in the other, a large sports drink.

"How sick do I seem to you?" I asked.

David felt my forehead. After asking if I was always such a baby when sick, he brought a bowl of ice water and a washcloth from the kitchen. He dipped the cloth in the water, then pressed this to my forehead and rubbed my shoulder. Soon I fell silent and closed my eyes, drifting off while he played a game on his phone.

He must have set this game aside at some point to peruse the lesbian art monographs on the coffee table, because when I woke up, he was asking me, with a mix of glee and horror, "Oh my God, is this Betty and Wilma?"

"Is what Betty and Wilma?" I mumbled. David held up a thin book I had noticed several times in passing. Its cover showed a painting of two women locked in an aggressive sexual pose. One muscular woman, a redhead with black eyes, gritted her teeth angrily and grasped the second woman from behind. This other, dark-haired woman bent down and looked over her shoulder with an expression of almost grief-stricken ecstasy.

Somehow, in all of my days in the sublet, during almost every one of which I had looked upon and appreciated this image of aggressive lesbian sex, I'd never noticed that these two women were Betty and Wilma from *The Flintstones*.

"What do you *mean* you didn't notice?" said David. He sounded almost mad. "Every day you have been walking by a picture of Wilma Flintstone banging Betty Rubble."

I had no satisfying explanation. He had said, horribly, the word *banging*. Soon, lulled by the white noise of the fan, I drifted back into medicated sleep.

When I next woke, the sun had set. The enchanted, noisy Brooklyn night had appeared, as it always did, as if from nowhere. David had gotten up from the couch, I assumed because it was time for him to go. He had a long commute to New Jersey before returning to work the next day—returning to more campaigns, more bottled aspiration, spirits. But after rummaging around in the kitchen, he came back with a small capful of purple syrup and a glass of water.

"Drink this," he said. He helped me up. It seemed so strange that this man, who I would likely see maybe one more time in my life, and who I'd probably lose touch with after leaving New York for another year, bothered to lavish such care upon me. He would probably be back on his smartphone, back on that grid of abs and pecs and other parts, the day after I left. Then he said, in a gruff, impatient way, with what I thought to be residual anger at my not having recognized Betty and Wilma, "Let's go to bed." He led me away from the monograph, away from the empty soup container and the empty sports drink bottle, both now garbage—so this was where it came from—and into the bedroom.

"And you'd better not make me sick," he added. To which I, once again, could think of no easy reply.

My Life as Lord Byron

The Ghost and Mrs. Muir was on. We'd seen it before, but who can resist a romantic fantasy between a young widow and the ghost of a ship captain in a seaside English village? Certainly not my mother, who loved England, love, and ghosts. My mother communicated with ghosts regularly. This was such a matter-of-fact part of her life that I had taken for granted from the very beginning; I wasn't sure what I believed about ghosts themselves, but knew for certain that, whatever they were, my mother saw them, sensed them, and spoke with them. Stories about the ghosts of former residents alerting her to their presence at open houses for coveted real estate, chats with those who'd passed to the other side, etc.: these were simply part of the ongoing family conversation about multiple realities unfolding simultaneously.

"You know, I had to help this guy who died out there a little while ago," she said, waving a hand over her shoulder at the Puget Sound. I was back on Bainbridge Island between periods of travel. My mother was house-sitting the big waterfront home of some people who worked for Microsoft and had gone to Australia. She sat tucked into the corner of the sofa, wrapped in a blanket and holding a cup of tea.

"Really?" I said. It was the word that came out of my mouth most often on visits to the island, in a way that meant, "Please tell me more, and I'm also not sure what to think about this."

"I saw a crew out searching for him one evening," she said. "He was a diver for some official department. He'd gone missing."

"My God," I said.

"So I spoke to his ghost," she said. "He was very confused. Like, 'Whoa, where am I? What's happening?' He didn't get that he was dead, you know? He had a lot of cocaine in his system. I had to break the news to him."

"Jesus," I said. This was new. It could've made an interesting contemporary update of *The Ghost and Mrs. Muir*, which is about a woman, played by Gene Tierney, who rents a house on the English coast that's haunted by an irascible sea captain, played by Rex Harrison. She helps him write his memoirs from beyond the grave. It has a remarkable ending for a romantic comedy: in her old age, Tierney's character dies, united with Rex Harrison at last.

"I had to tell him gently, of course," she said. "It's best to be gentle with a ghost that doesn't know it's dead. It can come as quite a shock to them."

I thought about all of this for a moment. "So you helped a coke ghost cross over," I said.

My mother laughed. "A coke ghost!" She liked that. "Well, he was a good person."

"Poor guy," I said. "I wonder if a lot of divers use cocaine on the job. Are they like the long-distance truckers of the sea?" I later looked up the details of the case. My mother shunned the news, generally feeling it to be a conspiracy of negative vibes, fear-mongering, etc., etc. "Not in my home" was her attitude toward the news, as though it were a kind of pornography. (Lord knows it can be.) She was sensitive to the world, like me. And she wasn't wrong about the news, exactly. I, however, occasionally swung to the opposite extreme. I wanted to know everything, especially everything scandalous, criminal, tragic, everything indicative of human evil, folly, and misguided passion. "Evil and disaster are part of a well-rounded diet," I used to say to her, when I tried to persuade her to listen to the news. "They're part of the informational food pyramid." The diver, I learned, had been just twenty-four when he died of "salt water drowning" and acute cocaine intoxication. I had just turned thirty.

Ghost talk interested me because it often sidestepped the personal. Or, to be more exact, it seemed to me like a way of repurposing personal details in riddles, fables, and metaphors. The only times it rankled were when my mother said things like, "You'll know when I die, because I'll come visit you." Meaning, in other words: "Don't worry, I'll haunt you when I'm gone."

I didn't mind being visited by the spirit of my dead mother in theory, but it seemed like a potential violation of the well-protected private life I'd worked so hard to cultivate. Could one make a convenient appointment for visitations by one's dead mother, in the same way that one made sure to call every couple of weeks? Or did the ghosts of dead mothers know when to show themselves without making a scene? I had read that Oscar Wilde had experienced a ghostly vision of his mother on the night of her death across the country, so maybe it was just her Irish side coming out. Delightful Oscar, who wrote of Salome requesting the head of Jokanaan on a silver platter as a reward for her dancing. The subject of being eventually visited by my mother's ghost brought me back around to those images—those decadent Aubrey Beardsley drawings with their insectoid human figures, Salome feverish and floating on air, her eyes gazing deep into those of Jokanaan's severed head.

In any case, ghost life was a branch of my mother's supernaturalism that I rather enjoyed. Another branch, the existence of aliens, also entertained. On another visit I'd sat in a similar formation with my mother—her on the couch, me sitting across from her in a chair—but in my childhood home, which had recently been rebuilt after a freak fire left it half-collapsed and charred. I listened to her speak at great, almost trancelike length about Paul Hellyer, the ninety-one-year old former Canadian defense minister who around that time decided to announce that world leaders were hiding secret documents that confirmed the existence of UFOs and alien species. Aliens, he said, had been visiting earth for thousands of years; they were, he said, unimpressed with the way we lived, feeling that we spent too much money on military expenditures and not enough on helping the poor.

"So the aliens are leftists?" I said, throwing this into the whirlwind of my mother's speech about aliens.

She continued repeating and riffing on Paul Hellyer's claims, frightening me a little with her fervor, passionately agreeing that certain modern technologies, such as the Kevlar vest and LED light, had been helped into existence by aliens. Certain species of aliens, according to Hellyer, passed for human, among them a group referred to as "Tall Whites." This makes me laugh, since it described me as a person. The "Tall Whites" were working with the U.S. Air Force in Nevada. Why was it that aliens always seemed to be pale and to prefer hanging out in the American desert? One rarely heard rumors of, say, aliens roaming Saudi Arabia or Sudan. And the public would have taken immediate issue with reports that a species of aliens known as "Tall Browns" wandered the planet, passing for human. I eagerly awaited the publication of the alien equivalent to Nella Larsen's Harlem Renaissance novel *Passing*. What American literature really needed, I thought, was an Alien Renaissance. Maybe it was already having one.

But far be it from me to discourage anyone's passion for aliens. Even I had my moments in that regard—I was only human. I'm not sure what's real or true. And, unlike Hellyer's aliens, I'm often impressed by the way we lived. Human beings built architectural marvels of storytelling around their beliefs; even paranoia, harnessed and applied with focus, can create mental hanging gardens of breathtaking sublimity, reflections of the human psyche at its most baroque. Stories, novels. Essays.

However, it saddened me sometimes to venture out onto the branch of my mother's growing preoccupation with past lives, which, having moved on from the coke ghost, we began to do there in the living room of a high-earning and absent family's seaside home.

"I've been thinking a lot about Lady Duff lately," my mother said.

"Really?"

I knew what this meant. My mother had been fascinated by past lives for . . . well, longer than I'd been alive. By the time I came on the scene—a story replete with its own significant paranormal touches, including an Indian guru who, my mother said, astral-projected himself into her bedroom to hang out with her while she was pregnant—her interest in things like hypnotherapeutic past-life regression and speaking with the dead was already firmly established. She'd experienced a crack-up shortly after my birth, owing, to hear her tell it, to a mix of severe postpartum depression and being overwhelmed by the wide-open, wildly swinging doors of perception. During that time my brother and I were briefly placed in the care of friends and family. My mother and I were separated for two weeks. I don't remember any of it. I've had my own crack-ups over the years, including a brief but intense and humbling one a couple of months before turning in this book. It runs in the family. It fascinates me. A relative a couple of generations back, pushed to see how long he could spend inside a hot tank in the desert during his army training, lived the rest of his life after that with a permanently fractured psyche. Another spent her final days in Ypsilanti State Hospital, setting for the book *The Three Christs of Ypsilanti*, in which a social psychologist makes three men, each of whom believes he is God, spend time together to see what they'll do. (They went on believing.) In any case, my earliest memory of my mom talking about past lives involves a skit on the children's TV show *Sesame Street* that reduced me to hysterical tears. I was a little boy.

Everything was unfolding like normal, the usual colorful, festive parade of multicultural puppets and humans living and singing in relative harmony—my mother wept years later when Jim Henson died—until a segment came on that terrified me. In it, confirmed bachelor housemates Bert and Ernie, whom I normally enjoyed, explored an Egyptian pyramid. (They naturally refrained from identifying this as a tomb.) Bert's Egyptophilic enthusiasm did nothing to quell the creeping fear of Ernie, who followed his companion with reluctance. They came upon two ancient statues that, eerily, wore faces identical to theirs. I became nervous at that point. Ernie told Bert he wanted to go home, that he was frightened, but Bert insisted on staying. He left Ernie by the statue to investigate a dark tunnel around the corner. Then, while Ernie's back was turned, the statue in his own likeness momentarily came to life, tapping him on the head with his crook. Ernie wailed in fear, calling for Bert, to whom he explained the source of his panic.

Bert sighed. "This statue here, made of stone thousands of years old, it tapped you?"

"That's right, Bert," said Ernie.

"Ernie," said Bert, nasal and skeptical, "Ernie, don't you think maybe you were using your imagination, hm? It didn't really tap you, you're just imagining it, hm?"

Bert once again left Ernie, that clownish imagination-user, who tried to talk himself down. With confidence tenuously restored, he said to the statue, "You didn't tap me, did you, statue?"

"Sure I did," said the statue, coming to life again, its voice echoey. Its laughter, uncannily Ernie-like, a staccato hiss, threw me into a state of terror. My screams and crying summoned my mother, who must have thought I'd hurt myself.

"What's wrong?" she said. "What is it?"

Afraid to look at the TV, I pointed at it, blubbering about Egypt and statues. "It came to life," I said, still crying. "It came to life!"

My mother held me on the couch, comforted me. "Shhh," she said, "it isn't real." Like many children, I was fascinated by ancient Egypt; I wanted to bring home from the library as many books about the pyramids, the Sphinx, and the pharaohs as I could. Maybe this supported my mother's impulse, at that moment, to introduce the idea that I may have had a past life in ancient Egypt.

I stood up next to her on the couch, holding her hands, and sniffled, curious.

"I'll bet you were a pharaoh then," she said.

Thus the idea of past lives became part of the family language—nothing unusual, really, just the taken-for-granted reality that one had lived before in a time and place other than this one, and that one would likely live again, live elsewhere.

For my mother, affinities for another time and place suggested a literal lived relationship to them. A fascination with Paris in the 1920s, as culturally prescribed or insisted upon as that fascination might be, hinted at having once walked through the era oneself. I have many thoughts about this. At my most critical I consider suspect the aspirational quality that marks many past-life fantasies—that and a certain received cultural nostalgia, modes of historical fantasy that limit the variety of lives we're meant to imagine we've lived. Patterns in past-life fantasies—much like fantasies about one's present life—have their own loaded preoccupations. They reflect our desires and our frustrations. Then again, I'm intrigued by childhood psychology studies reporting that, at a certain age, usually shortly after children begin to speak in coherent sentences and stories, many people have been known to spout uncannily cogent narratives that have the appearance of memories from another life. My former drag mentor Glamamore once told me that when she was a little boy she suddenly began speaking Gaelic to her mother and grandmother. And my younger sister had, in fact, told a fully formed and uncanny story when she was little, one that my mother says was a family memory from an earlier generation: a boiler bursting, a house exploding, everyone running outside into the snow.

So my attitude toward past lives remains a tangle: curiosity, skepticism, willingness to accept the limits of my own understanding. I'm a little bit Ernie, a little bit Bert. As with any instrument of human meaning-making, it gets played in different ways, sometimes virtuosically (as though it were, in fact, the one doing the playing), sometimes in clumsy practice or with suspect motives. Which brings me back to the open question of my mother and Lady Duff. Having broached the subject, she produced a printed copy of a photograph from a pile of papers on a folding card table by the window.

"It's in the eyes," she said, handing it to me. The photo showed Lady Duff Stirling Twysden with Ernest Hemingway and four other figures, all of them at a table in a café in Pamplona. The eyes of Lady Duff did, indeed, gleam with creative fire, a radiant zeal and lively wit that my mother shared to a certain extent. "Do you see it?"

"Yes," I said, "in a way."

There was so much I felt I shouldn't say. These past lives seemed important to my mother, part of a creative process of some kind. My sympathies lay with the creative process and my mother's relationship with it. She, too, was an artist. Her creative energies seemed to me to be funneling more and more into past lives in which she'd been a woman in the shadow of some legendary male author. Lady Duff, inspiration for Bret Ashley in *The Sun Also Rises*, was one; she'd also discovered that she'd been the wife of the Irish poet and songwriter Thomas Moore. Why not be Thomas Moore himself? Maybe, I thought, these acts of imagination amounted to a feminist reclaiming of sorts. Was my mother traveling back through time in order to liberate the ghostly lives of women who, flesh and blood and brains, were remembered primarily for their roles in the existential dramas of literary men?

Maybe the ephemeral form this creative energy took satisfied her, though. Maybe it was just me, driven by my fear of annihilation, who wanted to turn living magic into monuments. I wanted us all to stay *here, now,* in *this* life. (My mother and I later identified my terror as possibly stemming from those weeks of abandonment when I was three months old. Maybe her going off to be Lady Duff or whoever else felt too much like that traumatic primal separation for me at the time.)

"We're still trying to figure out who you were back then," she said. By "we" she meant the other seers and psychics she consulted regularly, and, possibly, the spirit world itself. "We're thinking Faulkner."

Though I'd grown outwardly quiet, I couldn't help but laugh. She said it the way one might suggest a holiday destination. Part of me didn't particularly like having my soul dragged through history with hers—it was hard enough carving out an independent place for myself in the world without being asked to believe that I was, at any given moment, accompanying my mother on an endless literary Grand Tour through nonlinear time. Maybe I should be more grateful. I don't know. I complained about it once when she claimed that I'd been around during her tenure as Thomas Moore's wife. I was the handyman who worked on their cottage.

"So not only do I have to escort you through history," I said, "I have to fix your house while I'm at it?"

She laughed, but it was as though she feared abandoning me in her time travel experiments. Part of me wanted to say, "Please, Mother, go be Thomas Moore's wife! I'm a grown man. I can take care of myself." Shortly after voicing my complaint, however, I was not cut loose from the fantasy, but instead promoted within it. I had not been a handyman after all: I had been Lord Byron.

The Right Honorable Lord Byron, notorious and strong-nosed. The mercurial, flamboyant mess of myth responsible for *Don Juan*, a poem of Oriental eunuchs, androgynes, and a hero whose decadent effeminacy makes him the object of lesbian desire in a sultana's harem. Byron, plagued by rumors and malicious gossip about an affair with his half sister, which, along with those of his homosexual proclivities—a taste for "Greek love," as it was sometimes referred to—drove him out of England. The role suited me fine: a bit showy, pale, dark-haired, full of unpaid debts and ill-starred loved affairs. I could live with having lived as Byron.

Only later would I learn that Thomas Moore—my mother's past life husband and Byron's literary executor—had, after a concerned, contentious gathering with publisher John Murray and several others, been present at the burning of Byron's memoirs. Moore fought against this injustice. He protested the destruction of the memoirs. Not hard enough, apparently: the opinion of those who found the memoirs scandalous and debauched prevailed. They were torn up and thrown into the fireplace of the publisher's home on Albemarle Street in Piccadilly. Now they will never be read.

Like God

The struggle to stake a claim to life independent of one's family can be slow and painful, not to mention mortifying. It can drag out into a messy drama marked by acts of crazed ingratitude, inarticulate gestures of revolt, and passionate rejections of privileged opportunity. In my case, it can leave you nineteen and slumped on a corner of a winding street in Barcelona, far from the idyllic Pacific Northwest island where you grew up, telling a stranger who's asking you for change—lying to them—that you're the wrong person to ask because you're homeless.

What you'll say is this: that you're *sin hogar*. You'll have looked this up in a Spanish-English pocket dictionary while lying in your bed at a hostel on the brink of summer two days after arriving in the city late in the evening, after checking into a bed-and-breakfast for one night and noticing, as you showered and shaved, that a few small insects seemed to be crawling around in the hair on your inner thigh. This will seem a little incompatible with the two months you've just spent first driving around Provence visiting important Cathar historical sights and then studying life drawing in Florence, though in keeping with the degenerate turn your study abroad program took in the eleventh hour—the smoking of Marlboro Reds and the frequenting of dark back rooms in basement gay bars. It will go well with the spell you're under, the spell cast by *The Flowers of Evil, A Season in Hell, The Thief's Journal:* the lice, the crabs, they'll feel like an invitation to keep going, a decadent welcoming committee. Symbols. You'll try to get rid of them right away, but you'll still have them by the time you're curled up with your dictionary searching for words of decay, disintegration, dissolution. This will be a few months after your country first invades Iraq with their "shock and awe" bombing. *Desastre*, you'll whisper to yourself under your breath, preparing for a role you've come to Barcelona on your own to try out for. *Infierno. Vagabundo.*

It will be incredibly hot out. Europe, a place you've never been before (in fact, it's your first time out of the country, excepting Canada), will be suffering an infernal heat wave that year. You'll read about elderly people dying in their apartments. And when you go outside—young, lice-bitten, full of promise—to slump against a wall and smoke and practice your vocabulary of desolation, the young man who asks you for change will correct you.

"*Estoy sin hogar*," you'll moan, which literally translates as, "I'm without hearth."

The young man will look at you, puzzled. You've probably spoken as though you were a character in an old novel. "*¿Vives en la calle?*" he'll say. *You live in the street?*

"*Sí*," you'll say, your heart pounding. "*Sí.*"

He'll nod then, give you a faintly tender look before saying "*Buena suerte*" and dashing down the street. As you watch him go, the bottoms of his shoes flashing as he picks up his pace, you'll feel thrillingly full of deceit and, for the first time in a long time, understood, though you won't quite understand why. Not for a long, long time.

————

Our program was called "the Classical Legacy." After spending most of the year studying the course of certain ideas in European art history and literature from ancient Greece through to the early twentieth century, some of us traveled abroad together to witness, reflect, discuss, write, and draw.

We traveled, also, as some restless souls will do, to transgress—or to imagine ourselves transgressing. We carried copies of Robert Graves's *Classical Greek Myths*, sketchbooks, flat tin boxes of Staedtler pencils, varying competence in French and Italian. (Mine was strong for having only started studying that year; my most beloved professor later suggested I continue devoting myself to languages and so secure steady work for myself as a translator and interpreter. Like all the best and most practical advice I received in those days, I never followed through on it, instead finding it sufficient to privately celebrate and rejoice that someone thought I had the potential to become competent in any field whatsoever.) We rented cars and drove from Aix-en-Provence to Avignon to Orange to Roussillon, eating gouda with cumin and crusty bread in mustard fields, dancing to 50 Cent's "In Da Club" at a Senegalese birthday party, drinking Moroccan mint tea, and listening to angry bald Frenchmen tell us we were fools for electing George W. Bush, that we must be entitled and idiotic American pricks if they thought they would deign to speak to us in English, global lingua franca, even if they did know how. We fled attempted muggings on the boardwalk in Nice, where we'd been told not to walk alone at night; we wept at the way the light came through a stained-glass window by Chagall, marveled at the power and simplicity of Matisse's Rosary Chapel. A falling-out took place between young women with beautiful, pastoral names—Heather, Amber, Fawn—and we ate bouillabaisse with fish heads floating in our bowls, their eyes small and boiled white, staring.

After that, the train to Firenze, all those rainbow PACE flags hanging from people's balconies on the other side of the border. There we played piano in the lobby of Studio Arts Center International and the program coordinator, a short, blond Italian woman, told us we had a gift for music. What were we to do with all these God-forsaken *gifts*? We smoked by bedroom windows in a big, shared apartment, bought a cheap radio, and sat on the steps of the Duomo waiting to hear again that Brazilian pop song "Já Sei Namorar." We went to life-drawing class and had break-throughs of perception trying to capture the play of light and shadow in the model's hair. Our beloved professor flew home when his surrogate father in America died (the beloved professor who once told you that he witnessed the mushroom cloud of an American bomb dropped on his home country, Japan, when he was too young to understand what it was, and that he thought that, whatever it was, its beauty was overwhelming) though not before filling a Ziploc bag with bay leaves surreptitiously picked from a laurel bush outside a restaurant. Women on the street taught us that the way to ask someone for a light was to say, "Do you have fire?" Men much older than us ran their hands over our backs in nightclubs, which felt so good it was almost upsetting. Shame, desire, violence, lust. We remembered we were meant to fill our sketchbooks and so the next day went looking for fountains to draw. And when the program ended, we went to Paris, to Toulouse, to Barcelona by ourselves. Some of us went home. Some of us wanted to erase the word from our memory.

———

Alone in Barcelona, I conceived a plan of attack: I would find a job and ditch America. Ditch school, mom, stepdad, brother, brother, sister, biological father-at-large somewhere; ditch shock and awe, Osama bin Laden, sexual repression. There was more to learn from the world than from school; within a year I could become enviably competent in Spanish, have untold exciting new experiences, stake a definitive claim to my own life. In the meantime, I would pay attention to myself and whenever I felt frightened at the thought of doing something interpret that as a sign that I *absolutely must do it*. That, I told myself, would be the way forward into the thrilling unknown, the path toward greater personal courage.

The first challenge that came my way was the entrance to a gay bathhouse downtown, at the top of Las Ramblas. I had walked by it before and felt my heart rate go up. Part of me wanted to know what was happening in there; another part feared reveal-ing that I wanted to know enough to go inside. Looking back over my teens and twenties, it's clear that the mystery of what men were up to in private commanded an almost overpowering erotic force for me. Maybe if I went into the bathhouse I might correct or resolve having grown up without my father. It will reveal a lot about the state of my psyche at the time that I came to believe, without comprehending that I did, the following: that one of the things men must be doing in their most profoundly private hours—that is, when not under my observation—must be making love to each other. Which is to say: loving not me but some other man. The fear I felt when passing the door of the bathhouse downtown was in part the fear, I see now, of walking into the shadows and finding my father there, his arms around another "son."

During all this time my actual biological father was working in an herbal apothecary in Seattle and then a hardware store in Port Angeles, working his way through a series of women who bore some resemblance to my mother. (I know this because of the one time, as a teenager, that I visited the apothecary with my friend Rachel, wondering if I might catch a glimpse of him. Instead, a woman who looked a lot like my mother manned the counter. I'd heard he worked there with his girlfriend.) He died a couple of years ago, so he'll never read this or anything else I write—not that he necessarily would have anyway; it took me two years to find out he'd died—and never know that on one of the days he lived and breathed and probably smoked weed (and gave his love to someone else), his estranged son, whom he'd met only once, the estranged son whom he'd told that his mother had tricked him into getting her pregnant (a lie) and then offered to smoke him out, was two thousand miles away working up the nerve to walk into a gay sauna.

It was my bad luck that, after some initial casing of the territory, the first older man whom I let caress me, into whose arms I fell and whose lips I kissed, whose body I started to grope, would be another American. I only learned this after we had retired to a private room to have sex, at which point our passionate grappling started to escalate until, frightened, I told him *solo los manos*—only our hands. He said, in plainspoken English, and with a tenderness that almost brings a tear to my eye today, "Okay—that's okay. We don't have to do anything you don't want to do." We carried on kissing and touching each other until, a minute later, he said, "Is it because you're positive?"

I shook my head. "No," I said, "It's just that—" I told him something true, though I don't remember exactly what: that I'd never been in a place like that before, that I wanted to know a person before we had sex, that I was afraid.

He held me then. "This feels nice," I said. He thought so, too, or said he did; God knows what was going through his head in those moments. I can only tell you how he acted, which through my eyes was with every appearance of kindness and concern. He must have seen how troubled I was; I'm lucky he didn't try to take advantage of my vulnerability for that reason instead, though, to be fair, I would have put up a fight. I may have been lost, but I never liked being treated poorly.

He told me his name. It's possible I gave him a fake one— I was pretty far from what I thought to be myself. "Where are you from?" I said.

"D.C.," he said.

We laughed at the fact that we'd both ended up in a room with another American, when what we both had clearly desired, or acted like we desired, was an encounter with some more exotic Spanish other. We talked about the city for a while, lying side by side, looking into each other's eyes. I'm sure we complimented each other's bodies, called each other *handsome* or *sexy* or *hot* and resumed our kissing and caressing, though it tells me something that I don't remember what any of that led to. Where this memory ends for me is with him leading me out of the room and suggesting that we take a shower together, with the two of us standing side by side, naked under streaming water, grinning and washing off, separate again but relieved somehow and joyful. That's the only part of the memory that I'm not sure really happened.

––––––

Around that time I was mistaken for a prostitute. This was understandable, since I'd been hanging around on a street corner outside the department store Triángulo with a group of young Colombian men who, I'd later learn, were in the habit of selling their bodies. I'd stopped to chat with them since I had, a couple days earlier, followed one into a bathroom stall at a movie theater—he had approached me in the public square outside with two tickets in his hand, asking suggestively if I wanted to see a movie with him; the one he ultimately selected, because it had just started playing, was an American movie starring Jim Carrey with the improbable title *Evan Almighty*, though it had been given the title *Como Dios*, "Like God," in Spanish—and had held his shoulders and caressed his neck while he crouched on the toilet, stroking himself until he came, at which point he'd said he had to go, gave me a kiss on the cheek, and fled. I'd watched *Como Dios* by myself, a lonely God. Now I'd run into him again and I thought, *Spanish practice is Spanish practice*.

I was about to get more practice than expected. While we were chatting, a guy who was probably in his thirties walked up and the others greeted him cheerfully, calling out the name *Sergio*. Then, in what I still consider a marvel of spontaneous adaptation and pointed on-the-spot social rearrangement, the younger men's hands fluttered here and there, now touching Sergio's shoulder and turning him toward me, now pressing my lower back and guiding me one step forward. Within a matter of moments, they were walking away, waving and saying good-bye, leaving Sergio and I standing alone.

Our eyes met. We had to laugh. Sergio didn't really speak any English. He said he was hungry and asked me if I wanted to go somewhere for a slice of pizza. He had a friendly demeanor and spoke in a way that seemed sincere. His tone and his expression matched what he was asking; this wasn't an invitation to "see a movie." A jagged scar ran through one side of his lip and onto his face. I said okay but still hedged my bets, adding that after that I might have to meet up with a friend. I did have a friend in town named Gwyn who was studying Catalan and linguistics at the university.

We told each other about ourselves over pizza. He was Colombian, from Bogotá, and had moved to Spain to get away from . . . something. That's why he knew the young men on the corner, he said in a certain tone, in what I would only later see was an attempt to establish that he was neither a prostitute nor someone who picked them up. He had a noticeable tic—a short, sharp, sucking intake of breath with his tongue pressed against his top teeth, which made a clipped *thh* sound. "*¿Por que estás en Barcelona? Thh.*" He cut hair for a living. He had a certain suspicion about me that I simply chalked up to my being not only a stranger, but a stranger out of context—an American student hanging out with a bunch of young Colombian guys on a street corner.

We did our best with the language barrier, and it may have been the effort we both made to listen closely, to learn about each other that in part led us, in our growing enjoyment of each other's company, to relocate to a bar and continue our conversation over beers. That was where he told me that the scar on his face was from being pistol-whipped by the Colombian secret police—or at least, that was the story as I understood it, gleaned through both description and gesture. Owing to my afternoons spent browsing the dictionary for words related to all kinds of damage and destruction, I knew the word for scar, *cicatriz*, and had asked about it, which impressed him. The reason why they had done that to him escapes me now, though I tended to automatically trust people who said they had been knocked around by violent authorities. There I also tried to explain to him in a fumbling manner why I felt I wanted to stay in Barcelona, to drop out of school, why I wanted to get away from America. Fumbling sentences about war. He thought it was a bad idea and couldn't understand why I would even consider walking away from an education. He thought it was a bad way to treat my family, that I was being ungrateful. "*Estás loco*," he said repeatedly, until finally I could only reply by saying that he might be right about that.

At the bar he also revealed that when he had run into me on the corner with the young Colombians he had assumed I was a prostitute, which was why he'd been so wary at the pizza place. Sometimes he ran into the young Colombians trying to establish themselves here starting with sex work. He worried about them, he said. From time to time he took them out for food.

Having fed on a literature of decadence and reversal in which criminals, thieves, murderers, and prostitutes were elevated out of the pit and held up as shining examples of transcendent transgression and holiness, I took being mistaken for a prostitute as a high compliment. I'm not sure he sufficiently understood or believed, once I'd convinced him that I hadn't been soliciting, that I wasn't *picking up* prostitutes, but that could wait; I wanted to convey to him a certain level of comfort with the reality of prostitution—though really, what did I know—rather than make myself ridiculous by protesting too much.

At some point he asked about my friend. I said she could wait. He invited me back to his apartment. I knew what that meant; I was interested. He lived near La Sagráda Familia, the architecturally incredible, psychedelic Gaúdi church the construction of which was still continuing to that day, seventy-seven years after Gaudí's death. The heat wave was still on and we complained about how sweltering it was all the way to his place. I learned new Spanish words related to heat. In his bedroom we had sex quickly, almost violently, though I didn't finish, and tried to explain while we were lying apart from each other, cooling off, that it wasn't that important, that I would next time.

"*¿La próxima vez? Thh.*"

Sergio found that hard to believe. But there was a next time, and a time after that, and a time after that. He would tease me when I left for the day—to wander the city and brood on my defection from home, family, and country while he cut hair at the salon—that I was going to see my *clientes*. It may have surprised him that I wanted to spend so much time together. But I really did—what I wanted more than anything was to get to know him better. That felt more urgent, more essential, more necessary to my soul than continuing an education in the classroom. This was what I wanted: to be out in the world, to connect with people deeply, all different kinds of people. New people; the people I already knew, my family for instance, were like shameful shadows trailing me. After several days, Sergio said it was silly that I kept paying for my bed at the hostel when I was spending every night with him. He invited me to stay. His roommate Ateneo, also from Colombia, had been consulted. Apparently he didn't mind.

So I moved in with Sergio. The heat wave raged on. I looked for work in whatever ways came to mind: visiting English-language bookstores, looking into tutoring. I had floated the vague notion of taking a gap year to my mother and stepfather, who naturally disliked the idea and wanted me to come home. "I'm exploring some opportunities here," I said. I probably lied and said that I was conducting said explorations through Gwyn and her network of local connections. In reality, I had met up with Gwyn once since arriving. When she saw me—she was one of my best friend's girlfriends, a lesbian; the two of them were the first people I came out to—she marveled at how I had evidently changed in the last couple of years. "You look so gay!" she said. Maybe it was that I had by then been shopping at European clothing stores and getting European haircuts, but no, it wasn't just that—she told me that it seemed like I was flowering, open-ing up, growing into a more self-assured identity as a gay man. I seemed less repressed and constricted to her. Somehow it made me uncomfortable to hear that, but I'd always admired what I thought was her uncannily sharp perception and intelligence. Aside from which, this sentiment encouraged me to share my plan of dropping out of school and absconding to Barcelona for a year or more.

I forget whether or not she approved. I'm sure she listened with interest as I maligned my family's fearfulness, conjured up a drama of needing to escape from them and from war-mad Amer-ica, too, of needing to *live*—romantically, recklessly, *now*. She had always encouraged me to follow my instincts and emotions in the past. That had never really been my strong suit. I was ex-periencing an explosion of self after years of denial as we spoke; I was swinging toward expressing myself at all costs.

That evening we bought a bunch of candy from a shop and ate it all, then felt terrible. We sat down on the street, side by side against a cool, shady wall, clutching our stomachs and groaning. "I feel like I just ate a bunch of clay," I said. Gwyn liked that; she joined in, crying out, "*Clay! Clay! Full of clay!*" Many years later, Gwyn, who had been vocally, militantly lesbian during her ten-year relationship with Rachel—she had always been the most vociferous about smashing the patriarchy and subverting hetero-normative convention—shocked us all by leaving Rachel for a man. Within a year or so she was pregnant.

Although Sergio continued to say I was insane for wanting to drop out of school and become a shiftless expat, and though he kept one foot in a practical and wise distrust of my intentions even as he inched forward into greater closeness and intimacy with me, he also tried to help. In short order I found myself with an interview lined up for a job busing tables at the restaurant where Ateneo worked. I found the prospect thrilling—I'd worked at restaurants before and had always liked the sense of camaraderie, the liveliness, and the moment-to-moment action.

My Spanish had been improving exponentially, too, I felt: Sergio and I could carry on bantering as we lay on the couch, wilting during the heat wave and watching *Los Simpsons* in our underwear. We could share pillow talk and discuss our occasional sexual difficulties and the feelings they brought up for both of us. We could share observations about each other and talk about fried plantains. We even took a day trip to Sítges, a gay-friendly seaside town, where we ran into a woman Sergio knew. She couldn't believe I was American, she said—I didn't *seem* American. I seemed *Spanish*! I left that exchange beaming and proud: I would've been hard-pressed to imagine a greater compliment at that time. To think that in a few short weeks I'd managed to be mistaken for both a prostitute and a Spaniard.

Drunk on this development, I showed up at the restaurant for my interview. The place wasn't open yet. It had a charming ambience: white tablecloths, gleaming glasses and cutlery, that peaceful relative quiet before opening hours when the staff is going about their preparations, their shuffling and clinking and other noises in the background. The manager sat me down at a table and started talking to me, asking me questions. I couldn't keep up, nor could I really express why I wanted to stay in Barcelona and work as a busboy in a way that was persuasive or satisfying to the manager of a busy restaurant. I *did* understand everything when he told me that he didn't see how I could work as a busboy if I didn't even speak Spanish well enough to know what he was asking me. I left feeling ashamed of my presumptuousness.

I'm sure both Sergio and Ateneo grew more doubtful about what my presence represented after that. Obviously, I couldn't expect to just keep living with them, an American escapee, a stowaway in Sergio's room. I'd had an idea, though, that had taken root after my first few days in Barcelona and that in fact seemed more in keeping with the general direction in which I imagined my immediate future moving.

Anxious but, I felt, mustering bravery, I returned to the bathhouse. At the front counter, when the attendant asked me if I wanted to pay the entry fee to come in, I said no. "*Busco trabajo,*" I said.

The man raised his eyebrows. "*¿Aquí?*"

"Sí, aquí."

Though surprised, the man told me to wait a minute, then went to find another man, presumably the manager or owner. He asked me if I was really looking for work there, and I said again that I was. He looked me over and shrugged. He said he could use someone to help out with cleaning the place.

You don't need very much Spanish to work in a bathhouse. The man showed me around the areas that I would be cleaning if I took a job there—the locker rooms, the place for towels, the laundry. I half-expected to see the guy from D.C. there again; memories flashed through my mind as we walked around. Afterward, he asked me if I was sure I wanted the job. You can think about it, he told me. Come back in a few days.

I had now pushed my fantasy to the breaking point. I faced a stark decision, one of two roads: either return to America to finish my degree or stay in Barcelona with Sergio and work at a gay bathhouse until I got on my feet. Though such a decision may look preposterous, and though I was not thinking at all seriously about the fact that I had no legal right to work in Spain and would unlikely be making enough money as an under-the-table bathhouse janitor to sustain myself, it felt like the most exciting decision I'd been faced with in a long time, maybe ever.

I used a phone card to call home and had a terrible conversation with my family. My mother started crying when I said I wanted to stay there, take a year off from college, and think about whether or not it was right for me. I told her that I'd been offered work at a health spa. My stepdad got on the phone then and tried, in more stern, measured tones, to make me see reason. I was in tears by then. "When I listen to you," I said, breaking down, "all I hear is fear."

Sergio found my stubbornness beyond belief. *Go home*, he said. *Finish school*. Nothing seemed right.

My courage failed me in the end. My family had reached out to my professor, pleading with him to do something, talk to me. He wrote me an email asking me what was going on; my family, he said, sounded very worried. *They live in fear,* I told myself. But I began to feel my resolve slacken. In short order a flight back to Seattle had been scheduled—in my memory my mother lied to the airline, told them there'd been a death in the family to get a discounted ticket—and I found myself being pushed into a cab by Sergio with my luggage. He said a hurried good-bye: *Don't worry. Finish school. I always thought you'd see that you had to return. I never thought you would really stay. I enjoyed our time together. Write to me.*

I called myself names all the way back to America. *Coward. Fake. Ingrate. Brat.* I cursed my family, cursed school, cursed my own failure to break free from what I was sure back then was a prison from which my soul had briefly escaped and was now crawling back to, keen to reinstate its own captivity. By the time I'd settled back in to spend the rest of the summer at home, I'd become both penitent and resentful. I'd brought back last-minute gifts, things I bought on my way to the airport and even *in* the airport. I gave my mother some kind of leather bag, nice but pretty obviously a desperate, last-minute purchase. She eyed it with disappointment, anger. My younger brother received a small book about Matisse paintings published by Taschen. My mother said it was probably not the best gift for him—a bit too racy, considering his age. When I revisit this with her recently, I recall her storming into my old bedroom and thundering, "I won't have this *smut* in my house!" She would *never* say that about Matisse, she insists—

"Art is *art*!"—and it's true that she has always been a champion of art, cultivated, a lover of art history with great, enlightened taste. Why did I write it that way the first time? Why did I picture, imagine, remember, dream up that which she would never, ever say?

"It isn't smut," I dreamed I said. And though I tried to make up for some of my madness that summer by working in the vegetable garden along the side of the house, pulling dry, dead clumps of weeds out of the earth, turning and raking the soil while American forces hunted for Saddam Hussein, the whole time I was thinking about everything I was missing out on. I could still be halfway across the world right now, I thought. I could be mopping up spilled seed and sweat, cleaning the tiled floors of the showers, washing and drying and folding the towels. I could be making a life for myself.

Tonight the Sea Is *Douce*

On the Saturday closest to my thirtieth birthday, I went out on the town with Andrew and Izzy, two of my Highbury flat mates. With my three months in dreamy Wellington, New Zealand, drawing to a close—to say nothing of my waning metabolic rate—the need to run a little wild at the end of an afternoon spent contemplating fiction felt realer than ever.

To this end our trio wound up, at three in the morning after hours of dancing, walking toward a Burger King on the corner of Cuba and Manners. This Burger King occupied the ground floor of a heritage building with an Edwardian Baroque façade. Once home to the first Te Aro branch of the Bank of New Zealand, the building now shouldered what the local government described as "considerable townscape significance."

"My uncle used to be the president of Burger King," said Andrew, sitting across from me and eating fries. The Burger King before us teemed with loud, drunken revelers.

"I can one-up you," said Izzy. "My grandfather used to be the chairman of the National Front."

"What's the National Front?" I asked.

"You don't know what the National Front is?" said Izzy. "Are you kidding me? Fucking Americans!"

"Look," I said. "I know about a lot of things outside of America. I can't know about all of them."

"You know what the Ku Klux Klan is," said Izzy.

"Well, of course."

"It's like the Klan, but in the UK."

"So the UKKKK."

"That's not a step up," said Andrew. "That's two steps down."

"Only two?" I said.

At this point, a red-faced, heavily slurring young man appeared as if out of nowhere and joined us at our table.

"I was going to punch you," he said to Andrew. Then, it sounded like he said: "I thought you were myself."

"You thought I was yourself?" said Andrew.

"I was going to punch you," he repeated. "I thought you were Marcelle."

"Oh," said Andrew. "Who's Marcelle?"

The young man set his burger down on the table. It looked like it had been rewrapped in its greasy paper after a brief manhandling. He hunched over it. "I can't even eat this," he said. "It's . . . look at it."

"It's sickening," I said. "I already regret eating mine." Regret had not yet crossed my mind, but this seemed a better direction for the conversation than punching. "It's basically garbage," I added.

The young man indulged in a drunk little chuckle. "I might get sick."

"Don't do that," said Andrew.

"Don't get sick," said Izzy.

"You're fine," I said.

"Just don't *push* me," he said, swaying, "and I won't throw up."

"So," I said, "this is where everyone ends up at the end of the night, after all the bars close. Do people hook up here? Like if they didn't meet anyone at the bar?"

Izzy said something about sex and death at Burger King.

"Look at this thing," said the young drunk. He unwrapped the burger, revealing a half-crushed, collapsing stack of seeded bun, mayo, meat, lettuce, angry yellow cheese. (I expected to see a slice of fuchsia beetroot, the surprise ingredient in many New Zealand burgers.) He recoiled, closing his eyes tight. "I can't even look at it!"

"It's like a circle of life in here," I said. "Sex, death, garbage, eating . . ."

"Birth," said Izzy.

"Sex, death, garbage, eating, birth," I said.

"I took a bite of it and now I have the taste in my mouth," said the young man. "It's horrible."

"It's garbage," I said. "It has zero nutritional value. We've all come here at the end of the night and paid to fill our bodies with garbage in this beautiful former bank."

"People so hungry," said the young man, glaring around the Burger King. "People so hungry they'll eat the face off your head."

"Why are we doing this?" I said. "What are we doing with our lives?"

"Hey," said Andrew, addressing the young man and pointing out Izzy's black vinyl bag on the chair next to him. "What do you think of this bag?"

The young man gave the bag a long look, then shook his head. "I'm not even dealing with that bag right now," he said.

———

I spent part of my actual thirtieth birthday, two days later, refining my travel itinerary. New Zealand had been good to me, but the time was nigh to move on to other, more chaotic cityscapes: Jakarta, Singapore, a giant Mardi Gras party in Sydney. A little more sightseeing remained on my Wellington list, after which it would be time to say, as the Kiwis at the corner stores so often did when I was on my way out the door with a bag of feijoa candies, "See ya!"

The next day, I walked down Tinakori Road, through Thorndon, to visit the birthplace of Katherine Mansfield. The beloved modernist described this place, in one of her short fictions, as "that horrid little piggy house which was really dreadful." Rather plain on the outside, maybe, but the interior presented a charming array of period pieces, reproductions, and sentimental bric-a-brac: family photographs featuring the beloved modernist, clematis wallpaper remade from a pattern discovered in fragments under the architraves, the doll's house that had something to do with her story "The Doll's House," and what I took to be a replica fruitcake on the dining room table. By the time I passed through the servery and into the scullery, I had become so used to staged inanimate treasures that I spent a long time staring at the sodden pillow of a tea bag in the sink, wondering where it fell on the spectrum of reality. The kind of tea bag I was staring at in the birthplace of Katherine Mansfield must not have been manufactured until the mid-twentieth century, well after the beloved modernist had suffered a pulmonary hemorrhage trying to run up the stairs at George Gurdjieff's Institute for the Harmonious Development of Man in Fontainebleau, France.

Thumbing through *The Letters and Journals of Katherine Mansfield*, I read:

"Tonight the sea is *douce*."

"The roaring of the sea was insufferable."

"I *hate* the *sea*."

Italics hers.

The way back to my neighborhood cut through the Botanic Gardens. Huge fern fronds cast strange shadows, and a crush of hydrangeas grew up white, purple, or periwinkle, I guessed according to the acidity of the soil. That's what I had heard about hydrangeas.

When I got home, I checked my email and learned that one of my ex-boyfriends had just died of a drug overdose. I had not seen him in about five years; we had definitely gone our separate ways in life, but the news still shocked me.

Dazed and sad, I made a cup of tea and sat out in our overgrown lawn, in the sun. The neighborhood at midday was quiet and still. My laundry swayed on the line. Nobody I've met in New Zealand has a tumble drier to go with their washing machine; they hang their rows of empty shirts, let them billow dry in the infamous Wellington wind.

My ex had introduced me to hard drugs. Brief but memorable introductions: crystal meth, cocaine, crack cocaine, heroin we smoked off pieces of tinfoil. We didn't date long— a few months, maybe, a messy, intoxicated dalliance. Sitting on the lawn, I remembered that he'd said early on that he had doubts about my *emotional maturity*. I was twenty at the time, he was maybe thirty. I'd just started writing for newspapers—small things. My ex had wanted to write, too, though he felt paralyzed by the examples of monumental, postmodern male genius he admired: Don DeLillo, Thomas Pynchon, David Foster Wallace. I don't know why, but I never responded like that to things that impressed me. Other people's work never made me feel like I shouldn't pursue my own. Maybe I was born this way; maybe it was another facet of fatherlessness, this feeling, sometimes, of relative freedom. Maybe I just wouldn't let myself feel the kind of awe that would make my own efforts appear fundamentally futile, frightened as I was at the thought of annihilation. Was I refusing to face the truth in that respect? Dancing over the abyss? Too much stillness freaked me out; I felt I had to keep moving, keep trying new things. It was its own kind of disease.

My ex's father had come to the States from Iran; their relationship seemed strained, though I never really knew that much about it. When I'd seen my ex a few years earlier, I'd been passing through Portland. He'd been making progress in a recovery program, having kicked heroin, and seemed pretty cheerful and healthy. Now this email. It was from one of his old friends. The friend used to perform in drag as Courtney Love. He'd tried to coin the label *dirt fag* to describe the grungy, gritty, aggressive variety of gay identity he'd taken on. I'd have to write him back to say that this was terrible news, that I was deeply sorry to learn of Keyan's death and how it had happened. I'd have to tell the friend that I was traveling now, that there was unfortunately no way I could make it to the memorial service, that there simply wasn't enough time. I was too far away. I couldn't change my plans.

Seven Sensational Party Spaces

The night before Sydney's world-famous Mardi Gras parade ("*I think it is the largest gay parade in the world*," a young German woman would shout behind me at the actual event—as if her sequined cowboy hat didn't explain it all), I'm in a three-level bar in Darlinghurst. Which, as the name suggests, is an absolute darling of a -hurst. It's also where the gay people who want to live in the gayest part of Sydney live.

I'm a few hours off the airplane. I'm having a good time. But the crowd, even squeezed in shoulder to shoulder, comes off a little chilly. By the time I've had a couple of drinks and the Justin Bieber song "Beauty and a Beat" comes on—which, to my surprise, and *delight*, sends at least several of the hundred or so men around me into a celebratory sing-along—it dawns on me how out of place I may actually appear. The men, though they surely must have flocked here from all corners for Mardi Gras, are clean-cut to a *personne*, reeking of meal replacement powder and Romanian dead lifts. Meanwhile I'm sporting a beard born of two months' neglect, a pair of sneakers that I may as well have grabbed from the top of the nearest Sri Lankan landfill judging from the looks they're getting, and whichever of my sad ensembles of neutral rags wasn't crying out for a beautiful laundrette at the dressing hour. I look like a suburban dad who stopped shaving after an unexpected layoff and wandered out of his house in the middle of a nervous breakdown. Maybe I am that; maybe I'm imagining everything.

In any case, it seems to be putting people off. The whole night I move from one floor to another, trying to cruise to music that sounds like it was produced inside a crystal meth molecule, trying to decide which floor is right for me when clearly *none of the floors is right for me.* Not one to dwell, being thirty now and basically on a high-speed honeymoon with myself, I set my discomfort aside and start dancing up on that third floor. Just as I'm getting into a splendid imitation of a gay man having fun in a club, some young thing wearing a T-shirt with more graphic design information on it than I can process tugs at my beard with both hands and screams, "Is this real?"

A question for the ages, barely heard over Ke$ha's "Die Young" played at tinnitus-inducing volume.

———

It's raining when I get to town the previous afternoon. I'm staying, to my own gut-tightening shame (*great* for the abs; ask anyone in Darlinghurst), at a youth hostel. I'm no longer a youth, per se, even though I still command the salary of one, and I'm only doing this so that I can spring for more line-reducing face belts and fresh air masks when I finally land in Asia. I make a quick dash out to George Street in Haymarket and into a nearby Vietnamese restaurant for some enlivening beef pho. Business is brisk, so I'm seated at a longer table where strangers can eat side by side.

There's space enough for another person to sit down beside me in hair-raising singlehood when a little wizard of a man enters, stage left, and sits down directly across from where I am. We say nothing, both of us now unable to look straight ahead lest we make harrowing eye contact. I'm disturbed by his outfit, which is a lot like the one I've pulled from my own colorless closet—slacks, a collared shirt, an aura of vague dread. He's also wearing a white palm hat with a black band. Months ago, in an attempt to branch out, I bought a nice white palm hat with a black band in a seaside town in New Zealand. I've been reluctant to wear it.

I left the hat sitting on my bed back at the youth hostel, but *I* know this fifty-something man has head-to-toe sartorial taste unnervingly similar to my own and I'm wondering whether that and our both dining out alone reveals something about who I'm going to become. I like to think that I would never sit down and maintain total silence directly opposite a stranger dining alone given the option to sit side by side. Then again, the window in which it would be precedent-setting for me to say something to him is closing fast and I haven't made a peep. Maybe by the time I'm nearly twice the age I am now I'll think nothing of doing what he's doing, and will even bring my hat.

————

After lying down in my bed at the youth hostel to recover from the Mardi Gras parade (I overhear the English girl sleeping in the bed above mine ask her friend, "Do you like what I've done with my pony?" meaning her ponytail, and the reply: "I love what you've done with your pony"), I rally and head to Moore Park for an ambitious after-party called Mardigrasland. The promotional literature for Mardigrasland promises an intimate gathering of just seventeen thousand people—seventeen thousand people in seven sensational party spaces.

Of the seven sensational party spaces, I spend most of my time in one, dancing through some mild back and hip pain that had started to bother me at the parade. A couple of hours in, I'm cutting loose with a handsome bearded man from Australia who lives in London and who seems to be around my age and his consort, a lithe blond woman in a cheetah costume that covers everything but her face. We're having a good time, dancing and smiling and having the hair cells in our inner ears razed by the DJ. Now and then my new friend pinches the bridge of his nose or rubs the heels of his hands over his eyes.

"Are you high?" I shout.

"Yes!" he shouts. "Are you?"

"No."

Later we're outside, sitting on the sidelines smoking, and I realize just how chemically transported the woman in the cheetah suit is. It seems she can't help but bare and grit her teeth, jaw clenched. When she speaks or listens, she leans in and her eyes become wide as specimens of the inexplicably large Australian fifty-cent piece.

When I tell old grizzly that I've been in New Zealand working, he makes an exaggerated yawning motion. "*So* dull," he says. "New Zealand is *rubbish*."

The cheetah woman leans close to me, her eyes straining to escape their ocular cavities. "I think you're a very handsome man," she says, taking my hand.

The conversation turns to France somehow, and I admit that though I've spent months in France, I've never set foot in Paris.

"Paris is full of cunts anyway," says he.

About now I'm wishing I had taken the half pill he had offered me earlier, this half pill of ecstasy that makes you hate Paris.
It would probably have soothed my aching back. Then again,
there's the cheetah woman, about whom he now adds, "She calls
her parents 'mummy' and 'daddy.'"

"Shut up!" she says. She drags hard on her cigarette, peepers
bulging anew.

"It's true," he says, "she's posh."

Before long, I excuse myself to catch a live set by Australian superchanteuse Delta Goodrem. Kissing the feline femme
fatale's hand, I promise to come find them again, to return to the
sensational party space where we first met.

———

By the time I'm ready to leave Mardigrasland, so many empty
beer cans and plastic water bottles cover the floors of the seven
sensational party spaces that we're all basically boogying down on
a raft of crushed recyclables. I've lost the clenched-jawed cheetah
woman and the hater of Paris in the sea of seventeen thousand,
and not for lack of trying to find them. I leave Mardigrasland
alone, just before dawn.

The next day I rest at the hostel. As true youths swirl around
me in raptures over their ponytails and, in one case, over how
her date was six hours late to meet her but it was okay because
he took her to a *posh club above a casino*, I fear I'm turning into
one of those unsavory characters that my own friends and I have
shuddered over in the past: the man who shows up at the gym
every day to lazily rotate his legs on the elliptical machine while
reading *German for Dummies;* the man with the bushy white
mustache who attends lectures at a university where he's not en-

rolled, using a ruler to take perfectly level handwritten notes. Aging, solitary men imposing themselves on questionable venues, hungry to improve themselves in public. And there I was, stretched out on an unmade bottom bunk in a youth hostel, elevating my legs because I had exacerbated an old lower back injury by standing too long at the Mardi Gras parade and dancing too long at Mardigrasland, eating gummy worms out of a ripped-open plastic package resting on my stomach, creepily writing about the twenty-year-olds with whom I was sharing a room.

The sun comes out in Sydney, though, the day before I leave. A pleasant stroll through the city, with several stop-ins at bookshops and cafés and art exhibitions, restores me. In front of a video installation at an exhibition called "We Used to Talk About Love," an adolescent boy in school uniform says to his pals, "It's not healthy," and one adds, "I'm a little scared." I spend a half hour taking photos for and with a chummy Peruvian tourist outside the Sydney Opera House. When he asks me, after asking me if I'm married, why I'm not married, I tell him that I move around too much.

Later that night I awake to the sound of the English girl in the bed above mine frantically falling out of her nest and staggering to the corner of the room. I open my eyes in time to witness her grip both sides of the tall, gray plastic garbage can, stick her head halfway into it, and retch. I pull out my earplugs in case anyone needs the advice of a thirty-year-old, and remind myself that tomorrow I'll be in Ubud, in what is said to be the beating heart of Balinese culture.

No Amusement May Be Made

I forgot my camera," I said to Wayan, the tour guide on our bicycle trip. He had moments earlier announced "Kodak moment!" as we slowed for our first stop—a lookout point over a mist-filled valley of tiered rice terraces. Two Swedish girls, two Dutch girls, and an English girl posed at the precipice, photographing themselves with evidence of having been to a beautiful vista in northeastern Bali.

"Oh, no," said Wayan. "Well, you will keep it in your head."

My head already resembled a home interior from the TV show *Hoarders*, more so now that the compulsive caretakers within had made it their mission to collect as many Indonesian words as possible. I knew the word for "beautiful," but lacked the impulse to document beauty. If I had to build a new mental wing to house the active volcano Mount Batur, so be it.

It seemed I could not cement a solid habit of picture-taking, and in this way I failed the demands of our time at every picturesque turn, successful only in my failure to do the thing I should have, in retrospect, done—done for friends, for family, for Facebook.

The feeling left me as the day progressed. The Swedish girls took cheeky snapshots of themselves knee-deep in the mud of a rice paddy outside a small village. "Dirty feet!" they cried, flashing smiles.

"It's like a spa treatment," one joked, stepping out with wet muck on her calves.

Crouching down to plant a few sprouted seedlings, Wayan said, "I used to help my father do this when I was a boy."

"It must be kind of fun for little kids to be in the mud and the water," said one of the Swedes. "Like playing."

When we stopped at a coffee plantation, the Dutch girls took pictures of a caged civet, whose digestion and excretion of raw beans is essential to the production of expensive, earthy *kopi luwak*; pictures of old Balinese women in their family compounds chopping and peeling bamboo into usable strips; pictures of a five-hundred-year-old banyan tree. I would later persuade my fellow tourists to email me these pictures, so that I'd have something to show for myself when I returned.

At a particularly stunning view of the volcano, the English girl said to me, "Bet you wish you'd brought your camera now."

"There's a lot of things I wish," I said in my head, keeping that there as well.

"What do you *do* all day? Just sit around?"

The English girl had said this in response to Wayan's description of Nyepi, the silent day that marked the Balinese Hindu New Year. On Nyepi, the streets stayed empty and the people shunned work, cutting their lights and electricity if they had them. Entertainment and pleasure were supposed to be forbidden, too; NO AMUSEMENT MAY BE MADE, read one of the headings in a brochure from the tourism office. It was a day for self-reflection.

In Ubud, where I had checked into a homestay, big *ogoh-ogoh*—monstrous demon figures with snarling faces, sagging breasts, huge paunches, and splayed talons, each built by a different group of artists—waited in temples or on the street, parts peeking out from under protective tarps. These would be paraded through town on Nyepi eve and finally burned in a cemetery, a ceremony of purification and evil spirit-banishing.

I felt rather like an evil spirit myself some mornings in Bali, waking to a volatile mental whirl of excitement, confusion, and dread. This restless energy knocked around my head like a poltergeist, hurling perceived needs and whims and insults across the room until about midday, when the blunt reality of being in a new place eclipsed headier concerns.

Stretches of acute self-loathing, though, are a natural, perhaps even desirable by-product of travel. I met many variations on an *Eat, Pray, Love* theme in Ubud who might disagree: women and some men who wanted only to feel the wind in their hair as they motorbiked into their bliss, whose billowing pants and serene, smiling frontispieces suggested every satisfaction, whose lust for remedy drove them to many local healers, much processing, much groping of and after the idea of a more authentic life—a concept as slippery as a fresh fish, and eventually as fragrant as a spoiled one.

Bali is, among many other more important things, a prime destination for travelers who loathe loathing and who will spare no expense in their quest to scrub themselves of its all-too-familiar stink.

In any case, I would usually be on a rented motorbike by early afternoon, hightailing it away from Ubud to lose myself hours out of town, buoyed by the village kids who gave me low-fives as I cruised by, or by awesome temples, like the eleventh-century Gunung Kawi, with its shrines carved into a rugged cliff face and its clear, cool brooks. I might stop to eavesdrop on a group of musicians practicing the *gamelan*, or to eat roast suckling pig at some roadside market among chain-smoking, silent Balinese men, men who turned on me the same wary curiosity they might show toward a limping, three-legged street dog with its tongue lolling out.

————

One day I went for a massage. I figured it might help with my back pain, which had flared up in Sydney a week earlier. My masseur warned me that the massage itself might be painful, and before long, with his thumbs and elbows digging into pressure points on my upper back, it was.

As the intensity of the treatment mounted, I started to giggle involuntarily. I wanted not to giggle, but by the time he got to my legs I was convulsing with laughter, facedown on the table.

"What is your job?" he said.

"Nothing," I sputtered. "Writing."

"How does this feel?" He grabbed the spot on my hand between left thumb and index finger, and I nearly screamed with pain.

"*Bad*," I said.

"Connected to your head," he said. "You think too much. You writer, think too much. You write with left hand? Try relax."

I tried. Soon, however, I was laughing again, laughing so hard that tears streamed from my eyes. (I had a bruise on my thigh the next day.)

"Hurts?" he said. "Ticklish?"

"It's okay," I said. "*Saya suka ini.*"

"Ah, you speak Indonesian?" he said, surprised.

"*Tidak*," I said, meaning "no."

"You write for newspaper? Or write the book?"

"Both," I said, for simplicity's sake, though the thought of the latter undertaking was perhaps one of the least relaxing topics of conversation on my list at that moment. My laughter, rushing out of me like the mad cackle of a screen villain transported by his own evil, kept pace with the pain, and soon the masseur started laughing, too.

"You write for newspaper," he said, "say, 'Come to Bali, have painful massage here.'"

"'Don't come to Bali,'" I said I would say. "'Terrible place. Too much pain.'"

"'Come to Bali, have massage you can't enjoy,'" he said. Then, turning serious, he added: "First time massage with me, you can't enjoy."

"That's okay," I said. "Who needs pleasure all the time?"

He instructed me to breathe deeply, and with his thumbs pressed into the back of my skull, he leaned closer. Then, in a tone of voice one might use to cheerfully check in on someone and make sure every little thing was as it should be, he asked, "Are you suffering?"

———

Nyepi came, the silent day. I thought it might be pretty quiet around the homestay, but it seemed all of the other visitors had saved up their noisemaking for that day in particular. The walls of my room, made of overlapping strips of bamboo using a technique I had witnessed firsthand on the bicycle tour, did little to silence the rowdy sex taking place between my French neighbor and a prostitute he had managed to hire for the occasion. In the lingua franca of my native English, they negotiated extended rates for services and discussed, mid-fuck, how best to improve upon whatever apparently advanced sexual maneuver had been included in the bargain—a maneuver that was, from the sounds of things, proving more difficult than expected.

A good amount of amusement was being made. This seemed to me, if nothing else, a culturally insensitive way to spend Nyepi. And from another room, music and singing! The young son of a German couple downstairs threw a screaming, crying tantrum. One of the Balinese tots who lived in the family compound lost his composure, too, running in circles and making a sound like the revving of a tiny, angry motorcycle.

"Hard for them to stay inside," his father said when I emerged for tea.

The next day I would fly to Jakarta and, I knew, would get to gossip with the homestay proprietor on the way to the airport, to speculate with him about the Frenchman and his prostitute. The proprietor and I had struck up a friendly, conversational relationship that began with his showing me music videos of Indonesian rockabilly bands on his iPhone over breakfast. (When I asked him one morning if he had read *Eat, Pray, Love*, he said his culture was not a reading culture. "Gossip," he said. "Talking.")

Back in my darkened room, I threw myself down on the bed. *I wish I had a prostitute*, I thought, sighing. *Any kind of prostitute.*

I'd never hired a prostitute, though I had been, as I mentioned earlier, mistaken for one. Without a prostitute, I had to create my own forbidden amusement. I closed my eyes and pictured myself walking into one of the many healing centers in Ubud, one of the many body works or crystal consultants, and making a beeline for the resident guru. I smiled as the scene unfolded, now only dimly aware of the cicadas clicking outside, the Frenchman fucking his way into the Balinese New Year next door.

"Excuse me," I said, entering the shop.

"Yes?" said the wise man. "How can I help you? What is the problem?"

"I hate myself," I said. I announced it with good cheer, with the embarrassing royal bearing I reserve for fantasy, with what is sometimes described as "obvious relish." "I hate myself!"

That's how it began in my head, where all my snapshots of beautiful vistas are stored—pictures of Mount Batur, pictures of Tampaksiring. What happened after that, friend, stays between me and my healer.

A Stranger in Siem Reap

For a period of time in my thirties, as you may have surmised by this point, I developed a travel mania. No sooner would I land in one place than I would begin to scheme, in the back of my mind, ways of escaping it. I've never taken anything like a proper vacation: every time I board a plane, bus, or train, I'm simply executing one part of an intricate plan to rocket through multiple cities or countries as fast as possible, to burn through all my money immediately, thus returning to a state in which travel is, once more, out of my price range—a state almost as unbearable as traveling itself.

Plan is perhaps too strong a word. The travel guru Rick Steves would beat me senseless with a copy of *Asia Through the Back Door* if he saw my itinerary back then. After a short stint teaching in New Zealand, I had more money than I knew what to do with—more than a hundred dollars, I mean—and had decided to blow it on a high-speed, enlightenment-free chase through Southeast Asia.

I was halfway through my six-country course. I had spent a few days in the chaotic Indonesian megacity of Jakarta, dancing to American '90s music in a smoke-choked club, clinking beers with an old friend on a high rooftop bar that had, basically, no guardrail, and wandering the almost seven-million-square-foot labyrinth of Grand Indonesia Shopping Town. In the Cambodian capital, I had eaten beef with ant sauce and gone to a baffling drag show. I'd made out with a Cambodian pharmacist I met there who told me that he'd marry a woman in the end. On a shaky Cambodia Angkor Air flight from Phnom Penh to Siem Reap, I had nodded off every few minutes, jolting awake whenever we hit turbulence. Burnout already loomed.

That didn't stop me from noticing a cute passenger across the aisle on my flight to Siem Reap. He looked Middle Eastern—born in Iraq, I later learned—and around my age. He spoke French with an attractive Asian woman, his traveling companion. Their intimate laughter reminded me how lonely I was barreling through the region on my own. After we landed, this pair, Karim and Sylvie, approached me at the baggage claim.

"Excuse me," Karim said, "but on the plane, we were trying to figure out what you do."

"Me?" I was flustered to be seen and commented on. "Well, what did you guess?"

Sylvie hefted a rolling suitcase from the carousel. "I thought cinematographer. Something to do with the image, with composing the scene."

"I was thinking teacher," said Karim. A half smile suggested mischief—flashing visions, perhaps, of just what kind of lessons might await us.

"I wish I was a cinematographer," I said. "I'm a writer." Saying so felt like oversharing, as if I had confessed a psychological disorder.

The three of us shared a *cyclo* taxi into town. Karim said he was exhausted, managing in spite of this to add flirtatious shading to his words. "I just flew from New York to Shanghai to Phnom Penh to here."

"What *you* need to refresh you," I said, "is an eight-hour, twenty-five-mile off-road mountain bike tour of Angkor Park."

"*Il fait chaud*," said Sylvie, fanning herself. The weather that week hovered around a comfortable 110 degrees. As I hopped off the *cyclo* at my hotel, they told me they'd think about the mountain bike tour.

They showed up for it the next day. Karim and I, I thought, could certainly fall in love while enduring hours of biking over rough paths, sweating through our shirts and looking at one galleried Khmer temple after another in potentially lethal heat and humidity. I admired his legs as he pedaled, the hint of chest hair at his drooping collar, the enthusiasm with which he threw himself into this unrelenting expedition. As the afternoon wore on, we took available opportunities to bike side by side, chatting about work, family, travel. He horrified me by saying he had developed a shellfish allergy in his late twenties.

"I ate shrimp, crab, lobster, everything all through my life," he said. "Then, one evening in New York, I had this huge crab dinner with friends. Within an hour I started to turn red. My throat closed up and I had to go to the hospital. I can never eat shellfish again. Who knew it could happen all of a sudden, just like that?"

"Terrifying," I said. "I can't imagine life without lobster." But I was thinking that yes, one's vulnerabilities can shift in an instant.

A twinkle in his eyes suggested interest dancing behind the encroaching fog of fatigue. I hoped that if I simply continued smiling and asking questions about his life he'd get the message: I was too tired to sweep him off his feet, so would he please sweep me off mine? Whenever he fell back to cycle alongside Sylvie I hoped that some part of their French conferral concerned me.

Sylvie suffered mild heatstroke toward the end of the tour, nearly fainting, and took a *cyclo* back to their hotel. As for me and Karim, we found little to say in the final hour, perhaps too concerned with getting to the end in one piece. *When will he tell me he really likes me?* I thought. *When will he tip his hand?*

Later that night I met them for beers but felt so paralyzed by exhaustion—perhaps he did, too, or by exhaustion mixed with fear—that we ended up returning to our separate hotels in short order. He was waiting for me, it seemed, to act; I was waiting for him. Normally I don't have this problem, at least when it comes to sex. The pursuit of sex, which at times feels like it's all masks, all theater, can demand so little real exposure. What petrified me was that I wanted more than sex from Karim: I longed to fall fully in love with him, which is much more frightening—love demands that you rest in place offstage, endure heroic passages of time together, time in which one must confront, continually, the tired, the ridiculous, the warty actor behind the role.

I held my face in my hands as the *cyclo* took me back. I was spending the night alone again for fear that love might discover my devouring need of it.

Karim and Sylvie had convinced me to wake up before dawn the next day to see the sun rise over Angkor Wat. I managed, even though my every instinct howled for me to stay in bed, stay in hiding. Yet another *cyclo* carried us through the checkpoint and into the tremendous temple complex. Many other tourists milled about the grounds taking photographs, buying souvenirs, and wondering aloud whether or not the conditions were right for a really good sunrise. They were. Karim, Sylvie, and I sat on the lawn, bleary-eyed, as the glowing orb of the sun rose warm and clear, trembling and perfect, touching the tallest spire.

"This really was worth it," said Karim. "Look at that," he said. "*Look!*"

I looked at him, wanting to grab his face with both hands and kiss him. That would have meant to live, though, and in front of all these people. I only played at living.

We spent the rest of the morning exploring the temple grounds in a delirious state, giggling and striking absurd, sometimes lascivious poses in front of statues. I took a photo of Karim and Sylvie in flattering light. "For my mother," he said. Sylvie then took one of me and Karim; I put my arm around him like a friend. A troubling relief came as I felt our hours together quickly slipping away.

On the *cyclo* ride back to town—the last time I'd see him; I slept through the evening and left the next morning—Karim, unable to stay awake any longer, leaned against me in a doze. The side of his head rested on my shoulder as the rickshaw rumbled over uneven roads. Sylvie, in the opposite seat, her eyes shielded by large sunglasses, smiled, blessing this union—and perhaps still trying to guess my true vocation even as its comic mask grinned back.

On the Loss of Being Here

For Kokoy Guevara—2017

Dear K.,

    I'm watching a video of you skateboarding in the Philippines, where you were born and where you died. A friend skates behind you, recording your swift downhill glide. You weave back and forth over the long road's dividing line. You died after skating like this, struck by a motorcycle. Nearly three years have passed. *So why write now?* you might ask. I might ask you the same: What do you want from me? It's summer here, a time when the invisible world draws closer to the living, burning one, when the heat smothers me like the hot breath of some emissary from the underworld. This interview with death drags on and the days are long; I turn in abandonment to ice cream, to perfectly formed entertainments, to love, the unknown. I perish next to a box fan.

    rafts of music approaching the mindless
    tennis played poorly or passably well: sweat flowing

one movie after another—new or old, blood-stained
novel punctuation of the hours scrolling
my thumbs in mid-July summoning images of the Good,
checking the weather

Peace and stillness elude me, K. Can you tell me why? They're like twin girls skipping away from me, laughing as they disappear down a dirt road. Everything is changing. I dread facing myself alone. I'll succumb to anything that keeps me floating, cinders on the air.

———

May I quote you a few lines from Douglas Harding's *On Having No Head: Zen and the Rediscovery of the Obvious*? Harding was an Englishman, a spiritual seeker born in Suffolk County five years before World War I broke out. He died more than a decade ago near Ipswich. That's almost as long as a human life can be. He once wrote about discovering while out walking in the Himalayas that he had no head. "This is not a literary gambit, a witticism designed to arouse interest at any cost," he wrote. And then he wrote:

What actually happened was something absurdly simple and unspectacular: I stopped thinking. A peculiar quiet, an odd kind of alert limpness or numbness, came over me. Reason and imagination and all mental chatter died down. For once, words really failed me. Past and future dropped away. I forgot who and what I was, my name, manhood, animalhood, all that could be called mine.

And wrote:

To look was enough. And what I found was khaki trouser legs terminating downwards in a pair of brown shoes, khaki sleeves terminating sideways in a pair of pink hands, and a khaki shirtfront terminating upwards in—absolutely nothing whatever! Certainly not in a head.

And wrote:

It was ceasing to ignore something which (since early childhood at any rate) I had always been too busy or too clever to see. It was naked, uncritical attention to what had all along been staring me in the face—my utter facelessness.

———

"Good to see your face, Mr. James," you said to me.

"Good to see yours." A hearty, back-slapping hug in your mother's living room. "I can't thank you enough for this."

"Don't mention it," you said. You looked different in the Philippines: fitter, more sinewy. But then the same receding hairline, black hair swept away from either side of the part, the same stern look that could give in to good, grinning humor if the mood struck, if the joke landed. Your tone of voice changed then: goofier, a slapstick stage pronouncement that might put us both at ease over my sudden appearance in your family's home—planned, yes, and yet no amount of planning can fully dilute the strangeness of one person traveling long distances to see another for curiosity's sake, for the sake of friendship.

"Welcome to Manila," you said. I had been napping in your book-filled bedroom after arriving early. Your mother had arranged for a car to ferry me from Ninoy Aquino to the high-rise condo in Pasig. As we passed through Makati and then over a river, the crush of traffic—SUVs, sedans, motorcycles, trucks—entranced me, the way of things here so different from Jakarta or Phnom Penh or Hanoi, where flocks of motorbikes rule the road.

"Do you have any dietary restrictions?" you asked me, cocking an eyebrow. "Do you eat tripe? I want to make sure you experience Filipino offal cooking." Your aunt, who wrote a column for a cooking magazine, your mother, and your sister talked over one another in the living room, bubbling with ideas about what kinds of Filipino food I should eat on my first night: *kare-kare*, *sisig*. Mention of *halo-halo* and your aunt and mother switched from Tagalog to English to tell me about your sweet tooth.

"We used to mail him boxes of his favorite candy in Iowa," your mother said, her voice bright and triumphant. "You didn't know?"

"I eat everything," I said.

Among these cheerful women, you struck me as oddly placed for a moment: brooding, grave. I knew so little; we settle for so little knowledge of each other. "Good," you said. "I'm going to make you eat *balut*."

We all took the elevator to the parking garage and piled into an SUV. Cars, cars: you drove us to Café Juanita, where we ordered a feast, everyone in buoyant spirits. I raised a cold San Miguel beer in a toast to you and yours. You and yours toasted me as your guest. One delectable dish after another came to the table: squid stewed in vinegar, herbs, and soy sauce; *kare-kare* with oxtail, tripe and various vegetables stewed in a peanut sauce with *bagoóng*; *sisig*, which you described to me as "chopped pig's face"; and a fried whole Laguna fish, head on, accompanied by little white dishes of tomato salsa. Knowledge may fail me, but appetite? Never.

In the middle of the meal, you returned to your proposed test of my American squeamishness: *balut*.

"Yes, time for *balut*," your mother said, her face all play-cruel smile. She called one of the waiters over and requested that he run down the street to a vendor, buy a *balut*, and bring it back to the table. "Make sure you get a good one," she said. The waiter nodded, then walked out of the restaurant. He returned several minutes later with a duck's egg.

"Oh, shit! There it is," you said.

"You're taking real pleasure in this, aren't you?"

You cackled as your aunt cracked the top of the egg open carefully, peeling away enough of the shell to reveal the curled-up, slimy little duck embryo, its soft, beaked head resting on a yellow pillow of yolk. You Guevaras tittered while I scrutinized the *balut*. You explained that the liquid broth inside was amniotic fluid, which one was meant to slurp. And then you took photos with both your phone and mine: me holding the *balut* with an aggrieved look on my face; me hamming it up with the *balut* raised to my lips; the *balut* alone, ready for its close-up.

(A month later, the sight of these photos gave me pause. I appeared gangly in a collared, pale linen shirt that had a curious affectation about it. Did I think I was a character in a Graham Greene novel? Good thing I'd ditched the woven hat from New Zealand that would've compounded the effect. I'd grown a beard while traveling and in the photos I looked a little too wild and ragged, too thin, my face flush from booze and heat. These photos failed to reflect the figure I hoped to cut at the time: a presence soft as linen yet savvy, too, piratical yet presentable. A Traveler. Instead: eccentric, lost. In a fit of vanity and embarrassment, I weighed deleting them all, erasing each unflattering image of my face staring back at me. The fit passed, though I still feel I'd been, in some serious way, ridiculous.)

You grinned and took video as I steeled myself to eat. I drank the amniotic fluid in one shot. Good—comforting even, like chicken soup. Then I took the creamy yolk and the meaty, slightly crunchy embryo into my mouth and tried not to rush through chewing it up as you Guevaras all laughed and cried out with delight. You all even applauded. I smiled through my embarrassment. I was glad, anyway, that it brought you pleasure.

"I'm proud of you," you said, your hand on my shoulder.

"I'm going to need another drink," I said. We laughed. Warmth spread through my body. For the length of the meal I felt at home with your family. I made a mental note: wherever I ended up in the years to come, I must extend an invitation, must repay your hospitality in kind. The thought that I might get to do so one day—that this exchange of life, begun in earnest now, might continue—gave me a small thrill.

———

May I confess to you a few things about myself? I'm frightened by the future and by everything that's new. I feel more lost in the world with every passing year. This though I met a man I love and will be starting a better job as a teacher soon—a teacher of young kids, middle and high school—and will, with my new salary, finally move out of the mouse-infested shared apartment where I live and into my own place. So, you see: good things, great developments, wondrous progress, superheroes, onward the course of empire and fine dining. And yet I fear this forward motion is erasing me. The terror of annihilation strikes on the heels of well-being; my boyfriend could tell you about the times I've leapt out of bed in the middle of the night, suddenly shouting and sobbing, consumed and inconsolable, hysterical for an hour or more, rocking and weeping on the fine little yellow sofa at his place while he tries to comfort me, brings me whiskey. "Why are we here?" I'll say, blubbering. "I'm serious! *Why are we here?*"

Is it true what Montaigne, Big Daddy Essay, said about philosophy, quoting Cicero? That to study philosophy "is nothing but to prepare oneself to die"?

Hey, K.: is all literature prison literature?

Last month I spent three weeks traveling in the Balkans. Bulgaria, Serbia, Bosnia. The truth is that ever since I started traveling on my own—that trip to New Zealand and Southeast Asia, where I visited you—I have felt increasingly less sure about everything, including myself, my name, manhood, animalhood, all that could be called mine. Remember how, in one of those enormous air-conditioned mall palaces in Manila, you revealed to me your nominally secret life as an amateur boxer? You wanted to stop at a shop to pick up some new wraps.

"It's not really something I tell people about," you said. "Not many Iowa people know, anyway. I used to do it more. My family didn't like it. I train more discreetly now."

"Do you mean—do you really fight?" You had better friends than me in America, ones to whom this would probably come as no surprise.

"Totes, brah," you said. You threw a few punches, dancing around an invisible opponent. Within an hour you'd be behind the wheel of an SUV, stuck in traffic with me, talking about Kant or about the ghosts of fallen construction workers rumored to haunt the Manila Film Center, built on the orders of Imelda Marcos. "Filipinos are obsessed with ghosts," you'd say.

In Serbia I traveled with a sixty-seven-year-old retired boxer and bartender. A former pro heavyweight, he'd fought Larry Holmes, "the Easton Assassin," in Madison Square Garden in the 1970s. I knew him through the bookstore where I worked in New York. He'd moved to Belgrade to fight a legal battle for property restitution, to reclaim the mansion his father had lived in on Krunska Street until the communist government seized it. In one room of the otherwise empty twenty-two-room abode, which also lacked electricity and running water, Bob's bed, wrapped in an eye-popping rose-colored sheet, abutted a shelf crammed with books. Books on the floor, books in built-in cabinets. Old photographs, frameless, of European faces gazing into old cameras and posterity—*us!*—as though in their finery they had paused to acknowledge the great fog before them. A half-dozen flies made weird loops around the room.

A few days after coming back to New York, I woke up from a jet-lagged sleep to the startling sight of my own bedroom. For a few moments, I didn't understand where I was—I'm sure that happened to you at least once in your life. But it wasn't only that, K.: for those moments, which stretched on too long, I could not remember *who* I was. Where did I work? Where did I come from? Who did I love? And I swear to you that, although I saw my body lying before me, naked arms terminating in a pair of tanned hands, hairy legs in a pair of pink and tired feet, I could not for the life of me picture my own face. In that moment, a void. It wasn't until I jumped up to piss that it all came rushing back, set out hastily as though by a host receiving sudden, unexpected guests.

"Filipinos are obsessed with ghosts," you said. I'd asked about a roadside shrine of some kind, a small and colorful piece of ceremonial architecture made by hand. Had someone been hit by a car there? Someone's loved one? Ghosts preoccupied me during the whole trip: my friend in Jakarta, a journalist, sent me articles about Indonesians' "weakness for ghosts" before my visit there; in Hong Kong—next stop after seeing you—I took a self-guided tour of sites that played a significant role during the bubonic plague epidemic that hit the city at the end of the nineteenth century, which I was led to believe had left so many ghosts behind that nobody who could afford better wanted to live in the formerly stricken neighborhoods.

Driving out of Intramuros after our walking tour of that walled city led by the flamboyant Carlos Celdran, you asked me teacherish questions. (I'd visited De La Salle, where you taught, had sat in on your class. You introduced me as a guest, then proceeded with a serious lecture the subject of which now escapes me completely. Your students watched you in serious silence.) "What do you think?" you said. "What did you learn about the Philippines today?"

Celdran came to mind, dressed in Spanish colonial garb as he walked us through the Fort Santiago citadel and the baroque San Agustin Church shouting, "Walk this way!" He'd led our group to vantage points where we, dutifully following, viewed evidence of the damage caused by American bombing and shelling against the occupying Imperial Japanese Army during World War II. (I bought a T-shirt from Celdran advertising his one-man show, *Livin' La Vida Imelda*, about the notorious former first lady, taken by the brightly colored image of Imelda Marcos. Within the year, however, it faded so that the face all but disappeared, leaving only white.) To you I said, groping: this mix of histories—indigenous, Spanish, American, etc., what a trip, what a lark, what a plunge! Amazing. Incredible. Fascinating. Complex. And though I knew a thing or two about America dropping bombs on the Philippines, to look, to see, to really *see*, here, now—

"When I was a teenager, I just wanted to get out of here," you said. "I wanted to study poetry in America. I loved American poetry. I would go to the bookstores constantly and pick up every new book of American poetry or book about American poetry I could find. Now that I'm here again, I'd like to get a teaching job back in the States."

A night in June years before: you reading a poem out to a crowd on a lawn in Iowa, face half-lit by a bonfire. I confess your language perplexed me, K., and still does, though your gravity and the revelation of your private rigor captured my attention. I'm reading something you wrote now:

I had in my remains and therefore left beyond
each page how tired I was of the lightness

in having already left: I laughed at it and with it
as all around it I became those beginnings

I beat myself into, so again I was out of a time
one was read by and priced my beating:

And again I was peopled with the city I called
to confess for the loss of being here, and so

I swore to step off a roof I had made out of hiding
from a home I could never return.

Did you know your president is waging a lawless and bloody
war on drugs, that police and vigilantes kill people in the streets
with impunity? Don't get me started on our guy.

"In the bookstores here there are these cheap printed antholo-
gies of ghost stories submitted by, uh, regular Filipinos," you said.
You honked the horn of the SUV, passed a slower driver. "*True
paranormal cases.*" In National Book Store, you tried to help me
find volumes in English or with partial English translations to no
avail. I bought the ones in Tagalog anyway: *Haunted Hospitals*,
Haunted Campus, *Haunted TV Shows*. The idea behind the latter
delighted me, as it suggested not that someone's television was
haunted, but that the TV shows *themselves* were. As though a
ghost could appear within a rerun of *Friends*, a show you loved
for some reason. (I never followed it religiously, though confessed
at a barbecue last week, when asked to share a "weird celebrity
crush," that I had a thing for Jon Favreau circa his cameo on the
episode "The One With the Ultimate Fighting Champion." He's

sweaty in a gray tank top and loose black workout pants in one scene, punching a heavy hanging bag.)

"So complex processes can be haunted, too," I said. A game of calling out other potential titles began: "*Haunted Puberties*," "*Haunted Crime Sprees*," "*Haunted Friendships*."

One volume intrigued me especially: *Haunted Call Centers.* So many American companies outsourced telephone customer service work to the Philippines that it had eclipsed India as the call center capital of the world. Given the endless hours a huge number of Filipinos spent working in call centers, it was only a matter of time before they started filling up not only with customer service calls, but with ghost tales.

"A call center *is* a kind of crossroads," you said. I recalled my own years working in the phone room at the San Francisco Ballet, wondered if spirits had flowed through the lines as I shuffled seats and dates. "Actually," you continued, "I heard this story about a friend of a friend. She worked in a call center and was there late one night. While riding the elevator, she said, it stopped at an unoccupied floor and a man in full Spanish conquistador costume got on. He got off on another floor shortly after that, never having said a word. The woman was terrified."

Questions abounded about the logistics of haunting at a call center in the Philippines devoted to serving the overseas customers of American corporations. A ghostly crossroads that stretched across the Pacific—could the American spirit world and that of the Philippines intermingle, creating a kind of syncretic haunting scenario? Did hauntings manifest on the customer service calls themselves, in the form of faint whispers in colonial Spanish or Tagalog?

"I saw a Cambodian ghost comedy in Phnom Penh," I said. You turned the car down a tree-lined street, bringing us closer to the Jorge B. Vargas Museum. A lesson in the history of art in the Philippines awaited me. "It was in a mall. There were no subtitles. I wanted to see how much of the story I could absorb without comprehending a word of dialogue."

"And?" you said.

"It struck me how secondary language is when it comes to communicating the full force of a ghost story. The conventions of a ghost story are, I think, universal enough that I even wondered whether the imposition of language might've diluted the power of the film for me."

You wanted to know more, so I described the story of *Preay Phnek 4* (*4-Eyed Ghost*) in some detail. In a village, a mother dies. Pregnant with her third child at the time, she subsequently appears at inopportune moments to haunt those left behind, acting as a kind of spectral conscience, commenting with some comic flair on the vices and flaws of the other villagers. Male and female energies clash: the men try to banish what they take to be this vengeful female spirit, but fail repeatedly, as when the local shaman tries to drive her away using a sequence of shopworn wards against evil—a wreath of garlic, a crucifix that the ghost, bored by the shaman's efforts, simply tosses aside.

Still she goes on haunting them. She sits in the branches of a tree, singing an eerie lullaby that throws the villagers into a frightened, cartoonish panic. She gives a final speech, a suddenly grave confession or rebuke—part personal shame, part disappointment in the villagers for their inability to grasp her true aim—in which, ghost baby in arms, she insists to those gathered that she never had any sinister intentions. As symbolic emissary for the awesome and terrifying force of Nature, she never meant them the harm they read into her reappearances. She wanted only to rejoin her family—her husband, her motherless children.

It's too late by then: she'll leave them, just as they wished, for good. It's only the living son and daughter, closer because of their youth to the mysteries of the great beyond, who react throughout the film as though her visitations are a pleasant surprise rather than cause for alarm. (They're like the daughter in *The Ghost and Mrs. Muir* in this way.) And it's those two who weep most, grieve loudest, when their ghost mother fades from view, vanishing forever to their tearful cries of *mai, mai*.

Where did she go, K.?

"That's crazy, bro," you said. You shared some popular ghost myths and some urban ghost legends of the Philippines: the folkloric Manananggal, a kind of flying vampire who splits her body in half and preys on sleeping pregnant women, using her elongated tongues to suck out the hearts of fetuses; the White Lady of Balete Drive in nearby Quezon City, who died in a car accident and now catches rides from graveyard shift cabbies or appears suddenly in the rearview mirrors of solitary drivers. "And then, of course, there are the headless priests. People in the Philippines are always seeing headless ghosts. And a lot of priests for whatever reason—priests, monks, and nuns. I guess it's upsetting to a Christian people that a holy person might be killed before their time. So, like, there are hotels that used to be seminaries, but were converted after the war. But during the war, priests who tried to take refuge from the Japanese there were killed and sometimes beheaded. Now you'll hear about these ghosts all over the place: roaming the corridors of hotels at night, appearing on the side of the road, wandering school campuses and parks . . ."

"Call centers?" I asked.

"Yeah, maybe call centers," you said. "They say the chapel at De La Salle is haunted by the victims of a mass killing from World War II. Apparently you can sometimes hear people screaming there on a rainy night, or see a headless priest. According to rumor."

"Shut up," I said. "Have you noticed anything?"

"I don't go to the chapel, really," you said. "I've definitely never been there at night."

"We should go." Volumes of ghost stories shifted in the plastic shopping bag at my feet as you guided the car through a curve. My idea amused you, though in the end it joined one of a dozen passing notions you or I had about what we should do while I was in Manila, notions dropped in favor of less effortful pleasures—watching Brillante Mendoza films or *X-Men: First Class*, drinking in karaoke bars, hanging out with acquaintances of yours at Jollibee, where you tried to convince me that the chain made its burgers out of earthworms.

"Cheaper," you said.

What if we'd driven on a rainy night to De La Salle—named for the patron saint of teachers—and crept into the chapel? Picture us there in that dark, silent place, Chapel of the Most Blessed Sacrament, sitting in pews on opposite sides of the aisle. Unlit chandeliers hang in a row over our heads. The rain beats down on the building outside; we wait for the ghosts of war. Picture us giddy like young kids—frightened, too. My heart pounds now to think of the heart pounding, pounding because of something sensed, something felt: a flutter of motion in the corner of my eye. Could those be the screams of the murdered, faint inside the hissing rain? A figure in the chancel drifts before us then, cross-

145

ing the raised level like an actor on a stage. "Holy shit, dude," you say. You say my name. "Do you see that?" Its hands grope the altar, feeling for what's lost. Its headless body, draped in pale vestments, collared with a white clerical band, turns this way, now that. Before we know what to do, it's gone—gone somehow, though we never saw it vanish. We rise and we run, children afraid, thrilled to be afraid, saying in hot, astounded whispers, "*Go-go-go-go-go!*" We rush from the chapel and into the hall, laughing and panting, taking the Lord's name in so much vain, so many times, down the stairs and toward the doors. Who could believe our luck in seeing the headless, restless dead? Who could feel more alive than we do as we rush, rush from that haunted campus, out of a memory, a fantasy, a wish?

———

Yesterday morning, before heading to work at the bookstore, I watched the original adaptation of Stephen King's *Carrie*, part of a daylong marathon of horror playing on IFC. My boyfriend left in the middle of the climactic scene—all that blood, all that fire—to go box for an hour with his personal trainer. I kept watching on my own. I'd forgotten Sissy Spacek's face during that microcosmic prom apocalypse: covered in sticky pig's blood, she's no longer aware of herself at all. She becomes all sight—a sight so pure, a focus so intense that it gathers to a laser point of potent telekinesis.

Do you remember learning about telekinesis when you were young? I came upon it for the first time in the Roald Dahl book *Matilda*. To think, one might move things with one's mind! I remember going home after school that day and sitting at the kitchen table by myself. I wanted to see if I too had the gift, and so I laid a blank piece of college-ruled paper out on the surface before me. Little me in a Gotcha sweater, years from meeting or losing any lasting friends, frightened then as I am now. The white rectangle fills my vision: the blue horizontal lines, the fainter pink one going vertical, the three holes like voids punched down the side, its utter facelessness. "It was a vast emptiness vastly filled, a nothing that found room for everything," says Douglas Harding of that "hole where a head should have been." Tell me, K.: what happens if, forgetting myself completely, I become the paper and I slide across the table, fall off, drift to the floor like a leaf?

Yours, E.

Ghosts of Boystown

I used to fall for people too easily. Even in my late twenties, after a stretch of serial monogamy, after a handful of relationships that ended in either disillusionment, festering resentment, or a sheer idiotic need to continue running around the world looking for other, newer people to love, I could still be absurdly naïve.

In a gay bar in Chicago—one of my favorite gay bars there, a little neighborhood place—during a summer when I'd just moved to the Midwest, I wasn't looking for love. Sex maybe, nothing maybe, but love? No. A street festival was on that weekend—not Pride but a pre-Pride celebration. Lakeview and Boystown teemed with gay men drinking, eating ice cream, dancing, consulting their smartphones. (I hated that name, Boystown, but there it was.) I had mindlessly cruised and flirted here and there, expecting nothing, exploring the city, enjoying myself. Then I saw this guy in the bar. He saw me, and one of those instant eye-lock attraction things that you hear about—you hear about it happening, but think it never really happens—happened. With this strapping, solid-looking guy in a brown T-shirt. Short, dark hair, a lively look in his eyes. A lady-killer. A murderer.

I thought myself pretty solidly jaded by then. I had come to the Midwest from San Francisco, a couple of longer relationships, along with several subsequent flings and passing encounters, had left me with what I thought of as a somewhat realistic handle on what it meant to navigate the seas of romance, lust, whatever. Being more or less alone felt good; who knew where it would lead? Don't get me wrong: I retained an outrageously unbridled fantasy life in which full-bore Technicolor meet-cutes still played an embarrassing part. I still believed, on some level, that I might eventually meet *the one*, or *someone*, a nice man in a bar, at a café, at an otherwise tiresome party.

I felt, seeing this man, this Texan, that I might be about to meet just such a person. A charge crackled across the room. Both of us walked toward the other. He was kind of stocky, like he might play rugby in an amateur league. The physical chemistry I felt while standing before him nearly overwhelmed me. We both did our best to play confident, checking basic small talk boxes—proper names, place-names, et cetera—simultaneously surfing on a wave of thrilling subtext. Never had the words *Corpus Christi*, spoken aloud, excited me so much: the carnal body in *corpus*, the pleading cry in the *chri* of *Christi*. *Where in Texas? Corpus Christi.* He was saying the words, too, *Padre Island.* What about Padre Island? Was that where all the dads lived? When I told him I was a writer, his face lit up; he loved to read, especially books about American history. He had been reading a book about the Mexican-American War before coming to Chicago on vacation. When it came time for him to reveal his occupation—as it always does; all roads lead to So, What Do You Do?—he looked a little reluctant.

"Well," his Texas twang charmed me, "I have to tell you: I flip houses for a living."

I suppose a red flag should have gone up, or a reddish one at least, but it's easy to feel in the moment that true love, conquering all, can bring together 1) a man canny and opportunistic enough to make a huge profit in the aftermath of America's burst housing bubble, and 2) a man who had managed, up to that point, to avoid ever signing an apartment lease. Anyway, the house-flipping Texan bought me a beer. He squeezed my shoulder and smiled. I rubbed his arm, then started questioning him about the process of flipping houses. At some point during an exchange about the morality of buying up homes people had recently lost to foreclosure, we started kissing. How did it happen? Who kissed who? I don't remember; one moment foreclosures, the next a warm, mutually enthusiastic embrace. For the next hour or so all our attention centered on each other: we spoke excitedly about our attraction, laughed at how fast everything was happening, fell silent and gazed into each other's eyes. What was this? I wondered. Fate? It felt unlike any previous barroom pickup I'd experienced.

The Texan patted my leg and told me he'd be right back—he had to use the restroom. Before he went, he gave me a searching look, pleading almost, as though begging me not to disappear on him while he took a piss.

When seven or eight minutes went by and he still hadn't returned, the clear sky of my enchantment darkened slightly. I told myself not to worry, but time kept passing, bringing only a deeper chill to his absence.

I undertook a casual search of the bar, which, given the size of that single room, concluded all too quickly. I looked in the bathroom—no one there. No window the Texan could've climbed out of, no back entrance he could've fled through. Left standing with an empty beer, I had to ask myself: had I imagined it all?

No. The Texan, the man who flipped houses in the greater Corpus Christi area, had to have been real. How could he have slipped out without my noticing? I ordered another beer for myself, thinking he might return. At least a half hour's worth of time lay unfurled at my feet when I decided to leave. I stepped out onto the sidewalk. It was dusk, and the sky a fiery pink, that color smudged with ash gray. A soft, honey-gold light touched the trees and storefronts across the street. How real things appear when the light is changing. All the men milling around in it, smoking in it, talking by the window of that likable bar in it—my peers, I guess you could say; my contemporaries in gay life—appeared newly wild, mysterious to me. I might turn my head for a second, I thought, then turn my head back, see only wisps of smoke hanging in the air, a window pane quivering to the pulse of some distant gay remix, the spectral afterimage of one man holding another. Maybe I'd been the one to disappear: in a parallel reality unfolding simultaneously to this one, I'd gone mad in the bar, mad like one of my long-dead relatives. That was it: I was still sitting there at the bar in Boystown, jabbering now, my mind having shattered before the possibility of love. My mind was a church window through which someone had thrown a jagged rock, a broken scene of worship. Love, I thought, a Texan who flipped houses for a living, is standing before me, his hands on my shoulders, shaking me, asking me if I'm okay. *There's something wrong with this guy*, he's saying to the other men around him, to the bartender mixing vodka tonics. He doesn't know I'm God now—blind God, deaf God. He doesn't know that I can't see love standing before me, can't hear it shouting my name, a name I have at long last forgotten.

Designs

The first time I came to New York, I brought an undignified pair of pants with me. These pants, blindingly gray-white and tight-fitting, looked too new—like I'd bought them in a last-minute effort to look *nice for New York*. I bought them somewhere in San Francisco—along with a new pair of sneakers equally deserving of contempt—as a twenty-fifth birthday present to myself. My then-boyfriend Dan hated them. He had studied design at art school. He had an eye for things, a knack for suitable dress.

A couple of days into our trip together, a design friend of Dan's who worked for Martha Stewart Living Omnimedia gave us a tour of the company's formidable headquarters in Chelsea, in the Starrett-Lehigh Building. Inside that marvelous and modern full-block structure, marvels on a smaller scale: the Martha Stewart crew, surprise, kept things super-organized. When the design friend took us into a vaultlike room full of meticulously sorted cutlery, napkin rings, et cetera, he said, "Here's where we keep everything kitcheny we might need for a photo shoot."

I opened a wide metal drawer labeled SALT AND PEPPER SHAK-

ERS. Inside, an array of them in a variety of styles lay in wait for their close-ups. Other drawers and boxes held butter dishes, parfait glasses, strawberry forks. *So this is New York,* I thought.

Our tour continued. We passed by the Martha Stewart test kitchen and into the open-plan work area. When I asked Dan's design friend how often he saw Martha in the flesh, he said, "Oh, she comes in here with her dogs. You know, she can be surprisingly gruff. She swears like a sailor."

The image of Martha Stewart gliding into the open-plan work area trailed by a trotting chow and two French bulldogs, peppering the air with profanity, made me smile. I still dreamed of working in magazines back then and hoped to say "fuck" a lot in an editorial office of my own one day.

But I shouldn't have been in the Martha Stewart Omnimedia compound. In truth, I shouldn't have been in New York at all. Dan and I had only been dating for six or seven months. We wanted different things from life. He wanted to display ceramic owls by Jonathan Adler on his mantelpiece between frequenting terrific eateries. I wanted to read by myself in a squalid apartment and take frenzied, helmetless bike rides through town, doing as little respectable work as possible. Or so I told myself. He had—and still has, I saw him fairly recently—a flair for working regular hours at well-paying, design-related jobs. Back then I regularly abandoned gainful employment (and apartments, and boyfriends) and overdrew my checking account to stay up all night drinking with drag queens. In any case, when Dan took me out to dinner on my birthday I probably should have turned down his second, surprise gift: a card pushed across the table during dessert with the happy announcement inside that he was taking me to New York.

Dan's full-bore generosity made me uncomfortable at times. I concealed my immediate mistrust of this gift—what kind of person, I thought, gives the gift of surprise travel? I'd seen this kind of gift given on-screen before. It never failed to strike me as an outrageous gesture. It put pressure on the trip to go well, for one thing. It was also the exact wrong gift for my temperament; travel awakened my meanest independent streak. While traveling I needed to move at my own pace, meet new people on my own, explore and possibly disrobe with life beyond the faces and places I already knew. Over the years I've strained many a romance and friendship by trying to keep this instinct in check—in New Orleans, in Vancouver, in Montreal. I'll always remember that first trip to New York, though, as one of the most exciting ill-advised romantic getaways I've ever had the pleasure of suffering through.

It can't have been fun for Dan, either. After all, I brought those pants. Those shoes. I barely bothered to conceal my bumpkin status, exhilarated by the air of the city, the electric, propulsive energy on the streets. My wandering eye clocked knee-weakening specimens on every corner. I felt like Charles Darwin in South America, transfixed by an endless and fascinating parade of biodiversity. Dan wanted to go to the cupcake shop or to dine with his uncle at a celebrity chef's restaurant, errands that interested me only inasmuch as they created opportunities to observe more strangers. I was a bad boyfriend, really; I rejected the world of cupcakes. I called them "an infantilizing dessert." I met several of Dan's family members, meanwhile longing to tear away from the table, run into the streets alone.

When after our tour of the Martha Stewart Living Omnimedia compound we joined the design friend and his boyfriend for a dinner date, I sat and brooded through a conversation about other New York professionals they knew, all of whom had bald plans for vocational advancement. The design friend held up a connection of his, a woman who worked in magazines, as an exemplar of long-term planning and ambition. Apparently she had risen through the ranks of whatever glossy she labored for with dazzling speed and determination.

"I mean, she has a ten-year plan to become the publisher of *Vanity Fair*," he said. He spoke in a breathless way, in awe of the woman's fearsome workplace acumen.

"She sounds like she really knows what she's doing," I said.

"The thing is," he said, "when she says she's going to be the publisher of *Vanity Fair* ten years from now, I completely believe her." That was a little over ten years ago now.

I wondered how many other people on the block just then had a ten-year plan to become the publisher of *Vanity Fair*, an institution that, on a certain level, like all institutions, would remain essentially indifferent to whoever served it, even in the coveted role of publisher. *Somebody* would become the publisher of *Vanity Fair*—that much was certain.

My discomfort with the circumstances of my New York visit deepened even as my enchantment with the place itself grew. One evening, after Dan and I returned to the well-appointed little pied-à-terre in Chelsea that belonged to another of his friends—friends, friends, *friends!*—I couldn't sleep. Dan fell asleep easily, probably owing in part to how few stimulants he consumed, but I often struggled with insomnia. That night in particular a trapped feeling set in. I paced the apartment, glaring at things—photographic prints displayed just so on the walls, Dan's sleeping body wrapped in what I knew to be a set of sheets more luxurious than any I'd ever touched before—resenting this, this gift.

The likelihood of our breaking up within the year appeared all too clear. I crawled back into bed. After staring at the ceiling for an hour, I dropped off to sleep.

We met up with the Martha Stewart friend one more time on that trip. He and Dan wanted to go to some sort of professional design expo. I don't remember where it was or what the event was called—the International Bunch of Impeccably-Dressed Design People in a Big Room Discussing Design Objects and Each Other Expo. I wore the hated pants. Many well-designed objects, all forgotten to me now, stood on pedestals, soaking up admiration, scorn, and indifference, getting viewed through well-designed eyeglasses. The Martha Stewart friend, the friend with the friend who planned to become the publisher of *Vanity Fair*, produced a small vial of coke and a tiny spoon. Was there a drawer for tiny coke spoons among the other kitcheny things in the prop room at the Martha Stewart Omnimedia compound? COKE SPOONS. I took a clumsy bump, suddenly quite enjoying the world of design and design people. Dan refrained. He glanced at me with the air of someone trying not to look a little betrayed.

"Much better," said his friend.

The coke improved my mood. It also made me more eager to flee the scene and more willing to do so. I eyed the exits. Soon our group stepped out onto the sidewalk so that the design friend could have a cigarette. I didn't really smoke, but I wanted to under the circumstances. The design friend kindly offered me one.

Dan gave me another look. I drew close to him.

"I think I'd like to go off on my own for a while," I said. "Walk around a bit."

"Is everything okay?" said Dan.

"Everything's fine," I said. "I just want to be alone."

We agreed to part ways and meet up later. They went back into their design thing. I went off on my own, other thing—my wide-eyed, fevered, cupcake-hating thing. Alone at last, and with all these gifts—the quickly fading coke buzz, the cigarette for the road, the few more hours in New York. Gifts that I accepted in spite of everything, and that I now had on my conscience. But each step took me further from such concerns. I don't know what possessed me, but I was walking now—in those hideous pants, in those unforgivable white sneakers—as fast as I could. I rounded any corner I pleased. I turned down any street that called to me, going nowhere. Within minutes I felt light on my feet and impossibly free, as though I'd planned on feeling that way all along.

The Tingler

Now I'm back at the beach house on Bainbridge, where my mother is house-sitting. I go out for a run one lightly rainy morning—it's Halloween, actually. Movement fends off the dreadful sensation that the island is hungry to swallow me up, annihilate me. And so I lace up, pull the hood of an old sweatshirt over my head, and run along the road that serves the beach house. Relief comes only when the road feeds into a park, the park into trails that twist through the woods. My sneakers splash mud up onto my shins and calves. The woods—rain forest, really, full of wet ferns, thick-trunked fir trees, cedars, small frogs, branches bearded with bright green moss—resound with the patter and hiss of rainfall. Here I feel wonderfully alive, and like I am, for an ego-rich moment at least, mastering this place, this lush, sodden land, by mastering myself.

Back at the beach house I return to my downstairs lair, panting. I strip and shower, relishing the water pressure and the heat. I feel comfortable and wealthy inside this borrowed shower. When I step out, however, drying myself on a towel belonging to this family I've never met, and when I dress and go back upstairs, the strangeness of the circumstances returns to me. My mother and I are haunting this house.

All my inner gripes and worries, though, all my doubts and my compulsion to dissect, all of it melts away before the opportunity to watch TV. Though never much of a TV watcher as a teenager—anti-TV liberal romanticism had its claws in me then; SHOOT YOUR TELEVISION, a bumper sticker on my English teacher's pickup truck had read—I find lately that I missed it. Given half the chance, whether in a hotel room or a house-sitting situation, I binge on its offerings. Why, I plead with TV as I sink into couch, armchair, or bed, why was I ever cruel to you? What came over me? Come back to me, TV, I can change! Sitting in the Eames chair of the absent Microsoft workers, I turn the TV on. I find Turner Classic Movies. All-day old-school horror flicks await.

William Castle's *The Tingler*, starring Vincent Price, is on. I fall in love with Vincent Price as the movie gets rolling. Vincent Price, his voice shot through with a tone of thrilling perversion. I wish I could become Vincent Price—become a suave, prolific character actor most often cast in villainous roles. I wonder as I watch Vincent Price play the role of pathologist Dr. Warren Chapin (who discovers a parasite attached to the human spine, the titular Tingler, that feeds upon the fear of its host), whether I could ever have a side career as a screen villain. I would probably have to play the sort of villain who appears cheery and charismatic and well adjusted, I think, but who is then found to be a seething psychopath just beneath the surface. People long to be reassured that admirable qualities in others conceal shameful impulses, especially if those others dwell in the public eye; this Puritan-tabloid mindset supports a simplistic conception of truth in which the fallen state constitutes our shared, essential reality. The notion of original sin, I muse as Vincent Price removes the corny, centipede-like Tingler prop from the actress Judith Evelyn during her dead character's autopsy, runs so deep that even many of those who believe themselves atheists—or New Age pantheists—probably still think and feel by its logic, all unawares. The very idea of redemption feeds and grows upon it, much like the Tingler, which can only be defeated by the frightened screaming of its host, feeds and grows upon the fear of Martha, a deaf mute murdered by her movie-theater-owning husband, Oliver Higgins, who frightens her to death with what amounts to a series of elaborate pranks, knowing that she can't scream and will therefore succumb to the growing, eventually spine-crushing Tingler. At times, I think, almost all of popular American culture seems to thrive upon this same addictive lust for redemption—even that which endeavors to subvert its insidious laws often reads as little more than tantrum, which is to say a scream of sorts that shrinks the Tingler only temporarily. A prolonged shot in the film shows the silhouette of Vincent Price's gloved hands holding a monstrous, wriggling Tingler removed from Martha's corpse behind a surgery curtain. I think: redemption means regaining one's soul by paying for its loss with a life of virtue; more to the point, it means never really regaining one's soul in life, but devoting one's life to an ongoing penance, enduring temptation and making up for temptation with acts of virtue until death comes, a release. If the Tingler is sin, I think, then screaming in fright—an expression of that weakness taken for the true essence of humanity, taken for the truth behind any hubris, any stoicism, pride, self-regard, or "boastful" show of strength—is a form of virtue. It's one way of doing things, this screamful approach to the Good.

My mother returns to the beach house from wherever she's been. Choir practice, I think.

"Ooh, whatcha watching?" she says.

"*The Tingler*, with Vincent Price," I say.

She makes herself a cup of black tea, then joins me in watching the film, which is a little more than halfway over. "What *is* that thing? The Tingler?" she says. The Tingler has just broken free.

"That's the Tingler," I say. I explain the way the Tingler works and summarize the plot developments she missed. We laugh each time the Tingler reappears. It looks more ridiculous each time, more like the rubber toy that it is.

"This is too good," my mother says.

The Tingler escapes into the movie theater owned by Oliver Higgins. (In the film, the theater plays only silent movies.) There it seizes upon a woman's leg until her screaming drives it away; Vincent Price shuts the lights off in the theater and commands the whole audience to scream. At last, he and Higgens recapture the Tingler in the projection room. Price then puts the Tingler in question back in Martha's corpse, where it belongs, and sews her up. But Higgins, after confessing guilt to Vincent Price, dies once the reintroduced Tingler in Martha sort of reanimates her corpse, making it sit up in bed and scare the murderer husband so severely that *he's* unable to scream. "Ladies and gentlemen," Vincent Price intones over the black screen, "just a word of warning. If any of you are not convinced that you have a Tingler of your own, the next time you are frightened in the dark, don't scream."

And with that, *The Tingler* ends.

"Wonderful," I say, truly pleased.

My mother agrees. "Too funny," she says. After a few minutes of shuffling around in the kitchen, she recalls something she'd wanted to tell me. "Did you know that they're having a memorial service for Bob McAllister tomorrow?"

"I didn't know he'd died," I say. Bob McAllister had been a legendary high school teacher for decades, a champion of young writers and actors passing through his classes or theater productions. He wore wildly patterned ties and colorful Chuck Taylors. His truck bore the SHOOT YOUR TELEVISION bumper sticker. He had opened the minds of many students to the glories of the literary and dramatic arts with his passion. Meanwhile, he'd maintained a reputation for hipness, knowingness, a bohemian, even dangerous friskiness and rebellion.

"Lung cancer," my mother says. I recall now that he often smelled like stale smoke. The tips of his fingers were yellowed with tobacco stains. He had lived into his early seventies; my mother and my older brother and I all had him as a teacher.

"The service is at the high school." I'd taken a poetry class with him. He remembered my mother well, told me she wrote poetry beautifully and that she had memorably used the word *chatoyant* in one of her poems. He introduced me to the work of E. E. Cummings, to which I at first responded with ignorant outbursts of impatience, but came, through his guidance, to love.

"I don't think I'll go," I say.

A documentary about William Castle comes on as a follow-up to *The Tingler*. I'm keen to watch it. My mother goes upstairs to make some money by taking calls from people wanting psychic consultations. That all happens online now—psychics like my mother advertise their services on one forum or another, posting their personal sales pitches, then set up call times with their querants. Among her areas of expertise, as established earlier, is the power to help people communicate with intimates who have crossed over, who've died. She enjoys ongoing professional psychic relationships with some clients, while others seek her out for a single reading. She tells me before going upstairs to work that she's annoyed because a woman whom she'd told to end her relationship had left her a negative review online. "I didn't tell her what she wanted to hear," my mother says. The service through which people contact her is called Voices from Beyond. There's a caller ID system with text-to-speech in the house, so that when people in need of guidance call a voice intones: "Call from: Voices from Beyond. Call from: Voices from Beyond." The call is coming in now. *Beyond*, I think, *is a beautiful word*.

To the Actor

At the Strand Bookstore, the crush of holiday shoppers crowding the aisles energized me as I rotated from Carts to Info to Fiction to History, happy to guide people through the hellish landscape when they brought me a locator tag. (If you're looking for a book, an employee at one of the info desks will print out a little locator tag for you with the section and subsection on it.) Questions and random statements swirled by: "I'm looking for any biographies of Mariah Carey you might have," "I don't like books with sex in them," "She got shot in the head and survived. None of her friends has access to education." Though demanding my unflagging attention and courtesy, the day felt somehow more effortless as it grew in intensity. The threat of an overwhelming, giddy mania loomed; I was getting drunk on the fluidity of the hours, electrified by the continuous influx and outflow of people. On my lunch break I took the elevator up to the Rare Book Room and sat in one of the leather chairs, calming myself. I read a few pages of Carson McCullers's *The Member of the Wedding* and laughed over a passage in which Frankie thinks about the freaks in a freak show and about her own freakishness:

Frankie had wandered around the tent and looked at every booth. She was afraid of all the Freaks, for it seemed to her that they had looked at her in a secret way and tried to connect their eyes with hers, as though to say: we know you.

We know you, I mouthed.

After eating lunch in the basement break room, I began wading through the crowds to reach the mobbed front info desk. On my way I passed a man with a wildly determined look in his eyes; he had a small book in hand and was ripping out the pages in clumps, crumpling them, stuffing them into his coat pockets. Was he actually stealing a book one handful at a time? Because it seemed so incredible, I decided to carry on without mentioning it to anyone. I hoped one day that someone might do that to one of my books.

The first customer I helped at front info was a young man with an eerily steady voice who asked if we carried books on self-hypnosis. Then a tall, stylish, svelte Jamaican woman with a red head wrap appeared by my side, grinning.

"Do you have a book called *To the Actor*?" she asked brightly, with actorly diction. "It's a book by Chekhov's nephew! An incredible book—*To the Actor*."

"Let me see," I said. I found it in our computerized inventory and printed out a locator tag. "We do."

"Excellent!" said the woman. She clapped her hands together. "Wonderful!"

As I walked with her to the Acting Technique section, she praised the techniques in *To the Actor* with a manic energy that exceeded my own. "This book is a miracle, I'm telling you," she said. "*To the Actor* brought me out of my shell. It helped me learn how to play people of *low moral character*. People I never thought I could play—*thieves! Hookers!*" She let out a high, fluting laugh. "I am a churchgoing woman," she said. "And I said to my director, *give me the hooker part*. And do you know what? I did it well!"

Her own story of temporarily transforming herself into a person of what she called, again, *low moral character* astonished her. She shook her head as though it were all just too much to be believed, referring to herself a second time as a *churchgoing woman* and saying the title of the book once more: *To the Actor*. By Michael Chekhov—well, Mikael, actually. Anton Chekhov's nephew. I found the book, meanwhile mirroring her enthusiasm, saying that *To the Actor* sounded wonderful and that I, too, wished I could play a person of low moral character.

"Are you an actor?" she said.

"No," I said. "I mean, not really."

The woman scrutinized me. I thought she might tell me that, in fact, I was an actor, even if I refused to admit it—that it was written all over my face, that she could see it there, that I was marked. (This happened to me often; I found it eerie. Once I was in a Turkish grocery store in South Brooklyn and one of the clerks gasped to see me, asking if I was a Turkish actor I'd never heard of. When I said I wasn't, she refused to believe me: "No," she said. "You are him! *You are him!*") Instead, she continued to praise the work of Chekhov's nephew as she followed me back toward the front info desk, saying, "A marvelous book—a gift, a *gift!*" She then picked up a slim volume from the sorting cart, a book of mostly musical notation called *Song in Shakespeare*, and launched into a whole new line of voluble enthusiasm and conjecture, marveling loudly about music in the age of the Bard. At that point I said it had been nice talking to her and walked away from her mid-monologue. Other people needed my assistance.

For the following couple of hours, however, that electric potency around *To the Actor* coursed through me. We're taught to think of history as so remote, I thought—untouchable, really—yet the most unexpected lines reach us, sent out by some strutting character, some player on the stage of the past. And the lines still hold a charge, as evidenced by this woman awakened to the inner lives of *people of low moral character*, her whole being buzzing with energy sent down the line by Chekhov's nephew—who, I later learned, died in the mid-1950s (in Beverly Hills, of all places). That night I found a photograph of Mikael Chekhov online: Chekhov's nephew, an influential theatrical actor and director, stood wrapped in a snow-flecked black winter coat, a homburg hat on his head. He clutched some kind of terrier to his chest and face. Both white dog and Chekhov gazed toward the camera. The latter smiled in such a way that lines bunched up around his eyes and mouth, and on his forehead; his eyes carried something kind in them, something caring—a mild, loving attentiveness. Meanwhile, the little dog had been caught in an expression one might call regal, even haughty. Though perhaps this impression arose largely from the drooping, beardlike white hairs around the dog's mouth and along its chin, which looked as though they might be wet from playing in the snow. I wondered who Mikael Chekhov had been before and who he was now—where his spirit had traveled before filling up that body and writing *To the Actor*, where it had alighted after his death in Beverly Hills, who was walking in this world now with his kindness in their eyes. *It could be me*, I thought, briefly entertaining the idea that I might be gazing into the mirror of my past, locking eyes with my own soul. *Maybe I should take up acting. Maybe I should get a dog.*

One Hell of a Homie

I wish I could tell you that my first shiver of what is sometimes called, at a clinical remove, "same-sex desire"—the first confusing surge of yearning, the possible answer to that shameless question: "So, when did you know?"—took place when I laid eyes, cinematically, on some captivating and similarly alienated boy at a young age, or when some kindly, sweater-vested role model passed through my small town. Or maybe when a formative book fell into my hands: *Oranges Are Not the Only Fruit, Querelle, Babar Goes to Provincetown*. But no: the real Babar married his cousin, and the properly "queer" influences came much later. First there was the movie *Class Act,* starring hip-hop comedy duo Kid 'n Play.

It would have been 1993 or '94, depending on how promptly hip-hop buddy comedies made the move to television in those days. Just over ten years old but already dreading another school day spent studying the history of Bainbridge Island—my hometown, which at least I was learning had largely protested the internment of Japanese-Americans during World War II—or practicing cursive (as if, as I was convinced at the time, we would spend the remainder of our lives writing in just such a dandified, looping, somehow magical style, closing letters with "Your humble servant" and sealing our envelopes with red wax), I feigned illness. I emerged from my childhood bedroom in a fit of fake coughs, a green blanket wrapped around me, looking for all the world like a delirious inmate wandering the sanatorium halls.

"I don't feel so good," I said in a pathetic voice. I must have known this line from movies—the ominous utterance that meant certain doom for its unassuming speaker. The speaker, who usually ignored their not-so-good feeling, would soon foam at the mouth or cough blood into a lace handkerchief, or an alien life-form would burst from their chest.

My mother took my temperature. Even if the glass thermometer under my tongue clacking against my teeth as I rolled it from one side of my mouth to the other revealed nothing special, or if my forehead only felt hot from the anxiety of getting caught out in a lie, my mother erred on the side of indulgence. When I later learned that she had been a bookish and rebellious child herself and that she'd developed psychic visions and routinely communicated with the dead, I wondered if her lenience was purely sympathetic.

I got to stay home from school. But soon the power of suggestion, kindled by my mother's admission that my forehead felt "a little warm," that the mercury in the thermometer had perhaps risen a bit higher than usual, got the best of me. I began to wonder if I had fated myself to a worse sickness than I could have ever anticipated simply by saying "I don't feel so good." I had uttered a curse. I curled up on my sickbed, in my green blanket, now both pleased with myself for my successful deception and racked with regret for having deceived—an act of hubris for which I would surely be struck down and killed. What did it really mean to be sick? Can we alter reality with our lies?

Just then a light-skinned black man with a severe, towering flattop appeared on my TV screen, wearing an orange prison jumpsuit. "Yo!" he said. "I mean, hey!"

———

What happens when the school records of a brainiac dweeb and a got-attitude street tough get accidentally switched?

"*Class Act!*" sing gospel voices over a high-energy, funky early '90s hip-hop intro, the whole thing exactly complementing the font of the title credits: playful purple sans-serif names underlined with an informal yellow slash, an aesthetic that makes such an effort to be casual that it could only be premeditated artifice. (As a phys ed coach will bark at his students later in the movie: "Now get out there and have fun!") Today the aesthetic reminds me of Hypercolor T-shirts and the clothing brand Gotcha, the first year-round "surf lifestyle" apparel brand, which my mother carried at her children's clothing store, Island Kids. I was an Island Kid and my mother dressed me in Gotcha. When I was home, made sick from my own lies and watching *Class Act* on basic cable, I may have even been wearing a roomy sweatshirt with the word *Gotcha* printed according to the laws of a similar aesthetic, a slacker before I even had hair on my chin. To the background singers' repeated command, "*Work that body, work that body*," I would have remained in bed, playing hooky and preparing to watch a movie set at a California public school. "*Class Act!*"

This 1993 film, directed by Randall Miller, is a typical tale of mistaken identity and comic opposites. Kid plays an academically extraordinary nerd, Duncan Pinderhughes (a name that his counterpart manhandles throughout the movie: "Pincushion," "Pinderpuke," "Pinderpuss"), and Play a troublemaking street tough fresh from jail, Michael "Blade" Brown. Thanks to a collision between Duncan and the school's principal on the first day of school (the result of Blade giving Duncan an uncharitable shove in the hall—that first touch, the first violent brush between men that sets into motion a magic spell of entangled selves, of cruelly separated psychological aspects fated to meet, mutate, and, in my fantasies, make out), their records get switched, landing Duncan in a remedial grammar class, Blade in Advanced Latin.

One can easily imagine the way this unfolds—think, for example, of any other comedy. What took place in the paint-by-numbers main plot made so little impact on me that the details slipped my mind until I recently watched it again. No, what obsessed me most on that tender, faux-fevered day was not the quotation plucked from *Much Ado About Nothing* for a pivotal moment of hetero seduction ("I will live in thy heart, die in thy lap, and be buried in thy eyes"), nor any of the twisty dialogue characteristic of all mistaken identity films ("No, don't *be* me— you be you *for* me!"). What would ultimately live in my heart, die in my lap, and be buried in *my* eyes was a minor subplot concerning Duncan Pinderhughes's parents.

When Blade first shows up at the Pinderhughes residence to give Duncan an attitudinal street tough makeover (baggy, boldly patterned "gear," a few inches buzzed off his towering flattop) his very presence mortifies Duncan's respectable upper-middle-class parents. It also infects them with a paranoia that will eat away at them until the curtain falls—a fever beginning with mild suspicion and building to hysteria. Provoked by Duncan's haircut-related screams, Daddy Pinderhughes creeps upstairs to eavesdrop from behind the door.

"I know you're gonna like it," he hears Blade say. "Stop squirming or I'll hold you down."

"Will you stop blowin' me?" says Duncan, referring to the blow dryer. "It's getting me much too hot—oww!"

Shocked, Daddy Pinderhughes retreats back downstairs. "Have you ever wondered about our son's sexual preference?" he asks his wife.

"You know," she says, "I never really was aware that he had one."

They laugh the idea away. Off-screen, however, the Pinderhugheses' paranoia simmers. "Was that our son?" they ask, frightened by his change in appearance. Perhaps the mother goes on reading *Family Circle*, as we last saw her doing, though her own family circle has been pierced by this new and pernicious influence, this whiff of flamboyant hip-hop faggotry. That is, until the next encounter: Blade, dropping Duncan home after some attitudinal fieldwork at a dance club, says to Daddy Pinderhughes in passing, "You know that kid of yours? He's gonna make one hell of a homie."

Daddy Pinderhughes looks to his wife. "Did he say 'homo'?" he whispers. The mother recoils.

The Pinderhugheses, however—the Pinderpukes, the Pinderpusses—needn't have worried. In the final scene of *Class Act*, our decorous parents wake up to moans of ecstasy coming from Duncan's room. A telltale bed frame knocks against the wall.

"What was that, dear?" says the missus.

The mister stares ahead, glimpsing the void. "I'm afraid to find out."

He creeps down the hall, bracing himself to see the worst thing he could possibly see. He barges into his son's bedroom. He sees; all at once, his fear evaporates. The fever breaks. For there is Duncan on top of a woman, proving his manhood at last. "Dad! Uh, I can explain."

"My son!" Daddy Pinderhughes shouts, shaking with delirious laughter. "My wonderfully wonderful son!"

"Dad?"

"Are you two comfortable? Can I get you anything, young lady? A beverage? Anything at all?"

"We're kinda in the middle of something, Dad."

"Well, son," says the dad, "I hope you've got your *jimmy-hat* on." Then he dances himself out of the room. Down the hallway, back to his own bed, back to his wife. Relieved at last from what was, after all, mere sick hallucination.

———

The only pornography I could find on Bainbridge Island, through friends who had most likely pilfered it from their fathers or their older brothers, was limited to bedraggled *Hustler*s and *Playboy*s. While I usually felt lucky enough to lay eyes on smut of any kind, admiring the flour-caked thigh of a man in a hetero kitchen-sex photo spread got one only so far. The composition all too clearly favored the eyes of some phantom straight guy. And it would be years before the Internet came along with its easily accessible mountainous heaps of sexual fantasy, sexual reality.

I could draw, though. The flour-caked, muscular thigh—the thigh of a man who by now may conceivably require a cane to cross his own kitchen, or who may have even died in his own kitchen one day long ago, who knows (in which case, has he returned by now, become some unsuspecting somebody's past life?)—this thigh proved enticing enough to spur on a desire for more fantastic images of naked men at play. A few years after seeing *Class Act*, I started making my own erotic drawings. The drawings as I remember them were marked by a lively, unschooled hand and a sense of lustful urgency. They brought together malformed but well-intentioned men, men who would have felt miserably self-conscious in a Tom of Finland drawing but whom I loved all the same and whom I encouraged to do things that would have had Mr. and Mrs. Pinderhughes weeping into their hands.

My mother found these drawings hidden between my mattress and box spring (odd that any young person ever thinks this is a safe hiding place; on some level they must believe in the symbolic nature of that gap, believe they're tucking their adolescent contraband into an inviolable dreamworld). She may have wept into her hands, too, wondering how to approach this parenting conundrum. I don't envy parents, who of course have all sorts of hopes and expectations for their children, a great many of which will be challenged and sometimes even thwarted by them in the most extreme and wonderfully dramatic fashion. On top of that, they have to suffer their children's unrealistic expectations of them. In short, a Bermuda Triangle of expectations where even the most intrepid souls vanish in the mists of that endlessly mysterious vortex, family.

For my mother, important confrontations took place in the car. This policy of entrapment in motion soon became the standard for our biggest fights; if she wanted to have a serious discussion with me, my only conceivable escape would then be to throw myself from a moving vehicle. I must have considered doing just that when my mother told me that she had found the erotic drawings I made and kept under my mattress, along with some underwear I had altered and written on in suggestive ways. "Where did they come from?" she said. Shame and fury overwhelmed me: the space beneath my mattress was not an inviolable dreamworld at all. There were no inviolable dream-worlds left, aside from those which I kept inside myself. I held my silence until my mother, after some unsuccessful coaxing, segued into an entirely different line of questioning:

"Did somebody do something to you?"

She was asking if I had been molested. This definition ex-cluded any of the minor, abstract molestations of life, which had been relentless: moralistic films that showcased parents' relief at discovering their children weren't gay, the violation of youthful dreamworlds, being made to read young adult wilderness sur-vival novels like *Hatchet* while elsewhere some similarly aged child, some Duncan Pinderhughes or Michael "Blade" Brown, was probably studying Latin verb declensions.

It would be far worse to be molested sexually, of course. But I hadn't been, so these were the only molestations I knew—the ones that seemed to be beside the point. The subplots. My mother meant only to let me know that if I had been molested sexually, I could tell her, which would have been reassuring if I had been. That my erotic drawings might be a sign of private struggle in the face of ceaseless outside discouragement, dressed always in the latest, flashiest fashions, delivered through the loudest, most crowd-pleasing and unavoidable entertainments, was not part of the conversation.

And I was hardly articulate enough to broach it. In my revi-sion of this moment of personal history my mother and I talk about taking drawing classes so that I can become a better cre-ator of homoerotic art. Vocational training. I could have been a young entrepreneur! Then we talk about all that has been "done" to us in terms of daily psychological violence, since by the time anyone has reached adolescence, the only truthful response to the question "Did somebody do something to you?" is the affirmative wailing of a terrified person sinking into a pit of quicksand—followed by an exhaustive list of all the ways in which your mind, self-image, and morals have been shaped by the culture you live in. Culture is, by one definition, something that happens to something else. But being fondled and groped and corseted daily by your culture isn't the same thing as being sexually molested. And you can't say any of that when your mother asks, "Did somebody do something to you?"

"It was a joke," I said. Then I fabricated a story about how a friend of mine, one my mother didn't like very much, one who was a kind of adjunct menace to my other, less troublemaking friends, had made these drawings. He'd planted them in my room, I said. *I was framed!*

From where I sit now, resentful that I was discouraged from what might have been a very lucrative career—my mother could be relaxing in a beach house I bought for her with my substantial gay erotica fortune right now—the whole thing seems like a bad joke. I mean everything, the whole scene I've just described. Our lives are often at least partly composed of misunderstandings and untenable lies we invent to protect one another and ourselves from—what?

"A stupid prank," I said. Incredibly, we dropped the subject.

———

I hadn't actually planned on coming out to my mother. By sixteen I was just happy to have fallen in with a pair of lesbian punks at my high school. These lesbians—one of whom would much later leave the other for a man, as I mentioned earlier, while the other went on to become a piano tuner and one of my best friends—were the first people I came out to, repeatedly blubbering the phrase, "Nobody knows! Nobody knows!" After that I put most of my energy into becoming the best psychedelic electric guitar player I could be, a task I prioritized above telling anyone else about my sexual preference.

I also played tennis, since working as a pro at a tennis club was my backup plan if life as a guitar god who sublimated his erotic desires into kaleidoscopic works of musical genius didn't pan out. There was another young man on the high school tennis team, one more obviously gay than I was—also more obviously popular, well groomed, and scholastically accomplished. I once overheard him say that he only used Kiehl's skin care products. Whatever those were. He often spoke to his gal pals in French as they rallied, favoring controlled, refined ground strokes, whereas I played a rude, sweaty, confrontational net game. He seemed to excel at all things with effortless elegance, and though we never talked much, I found his ability to keep everything so utterly together nothing short of astonishing. But then I'd grown up wearing roomy Gotcha sweaters and pretending I was sick so I could stay home and watch *Class Act* on TV. He probably had his entire wardrobe handsewn by Ralph Lauren himself, I thought. Ralph Lauren probably mowed their lawn on weekends to make pocket money.

One day, I was standing with my mother in the kitchen after she'd attended one of my tennis matches. She commented on my teammate, insinuating that his flamboyant, effeminate personality was nothing to envy. "He's going to have a hard life," she said of the young man who later designed dresses worn by Michelle Obama.

"I think he'll be fine," I said. I walked out of the room.

Her presumption annoyed me. My mother, who experienced psychic visions and communicated with the dead—surely she had gay friends; was there such a thing as a closed-minded psychic?—was trying either to draw out my own confession or to engage me in a slanderous conversation about gay people. Of course, it could have been worse: I could have played along, and forever treasured the memory of my mother and me cruelly ridiculing the limp wrists and doomed futures of gay men everywhere. "God, why do they have to shove it in our faces?" I could have said to my mother, who, pleased to have found common ground with me at last, might have said, "Foolhardy faggots! How sad their plights will be, how devoid of any of the finer things in life, any of our hard-earned decorum or discreet aesthetic pleasures. And how hard it must be for their parents!"

Our big confrontation came not long after that, over, of all things, a permission slip. I was enrolled in a high school sociology class called "Culture, Power, and Society." (It may as well have been called "Did Somebody Do Something to You?"). A week-long unit examining homosexuality in popular culture meant that every student had to have a permission slip signed by their parent or guardian. It was the only time I had ever needed permission to study something, which made it more forbidden and exciting, just the way I prefer my homosexuality. Nobody needed permission to learn about trench foot, or about bodies heaped in pits, gassed, tortured, imprisoned, enslaved, broken, incinerated, blown to pieces, and bathed in atomic radiation. We, however, were going to watch *Boys Don't Cry*, or possibly *Love! Valour! Compassion!* And for this, permission was required—without it, some parents would have undoubtedly accused the school of indoctrinating their children. Their little girls would have started coming home with Hilary Swank haircuts, their little boys running off with seven of their middle-aged gay friends for an emotionally complex but ultimately life-affirming weekend at their lakeside summer vacation house.

A number of students disappeared from class that week.

In any case, I brought the permission slip to my mother. It was near dusk. The narrow hallway we stood in glowed with the rich, fading light of day. I seem to recall particles of dust circling in the light; what a pretty image, and how appropriate for a memory.

"Oh, here," I said. I handed her the paper slip.

She read it over and shook her head. Then she said something unpleasant about gay people, something provoking. I can't even remember the exact nature of the slander, because by then I was trembling, suddenly aware that I was about to do something I hadn't planned on doing at all—at least not for a long while; I had been waiting for the perfect moment, which, of course, only remains perfect by never arriving. After an uncomfortable silence during which my mother must have read me like an open and shameful book—a book you're not sure you want on display in your library—she added, "You would tell me if you were, wouldn't you?"

Our eyes locked. Bristling with a sudden desire to thwart my mother, I came out—for reasons of drama and self-preservation, but also, it must be said, to defy her. "I would," I said. "I am."

My mother burst into tears and ran to her room. She took to her bed with a box of tissues. I stood in the doorway, watching her collapse along with her expectations of me, watching the fever of her hysteria spike.

"You're in for a life of pain," she said.

Relief sometimes takes surprising forms. I found just then that I didn't feel like crying at all. Instead I started laughing. Laughing at my mother, upon whose fears it had suddenly become a delight to play—a relief for me. "Can I get you anything, young lady?" I felt like saying. "A beverage? Anything at all?" This was better than watching some gay movie, and I didn't even need a permission slip! While my mother wept, I tried to contain myself. I felt giddy and villainous; now that I knew I could make people cry by coming out, I couldn't wait to do it again.

"This is the worst thing you could have told me," she said.

That seemed even funnier! In part because I could think of so many worse things. What if I had told her that I was going to detonate a bomb at my school or that I had pawned my textbooks to buy the ingredients necessary for homemade crystal meth? What if I had told her that I was in a relationship with one of my female teachers, like what had just happened with that thirteen-year-old boy and his teacher Mary Kay Letourneau in nearby Des Moines, Washington? Or, what if I told her that I had gotten my teenage girlfriend pregnant, that we were going to keep the baby and name it—I don't know, Blade?

Who can say for sure. Nothing ever happens how I think it will. Maybe my mother would have discovered that she needn't have worried. Fever would break, fear evaporate. Maybe she would have started laughing, overjoyed, and cried, "My son! My wonderfully wonderful son!" Then, relieved at last from paranoia, from mere sick hallucination, she might have done what they do in movies—one of those many half-forgotten, interchangeable movies—and, a regular Mr. Pinderhughes, danced herself out of the room.

Natural Lives

Shortly after relocating from Iowa to Brooklyn—and discovering I lived a block away from a street named Albemarle, the name of the street in central London where the only copy of Lord Byron's memoirs were burned—I landed that aforementioned job at the Strand, the giant independent bookstore. I had a couple of days to prepare but soon realized it required no preparation at all. I curled up on my air mattress, smartphone in hand, and started exchanging app messages with men in my neighborhood, expecting nothing.

A guy whom I'll call Sam eventually took an interest. Sam was tall, handsome, dark-skinned, very chatty via text. His profile photos appealed: here he leaned forward with a smile while sitting on a boat at sea somewhere, elbows resting on knees; here he smiled for the camera, dressed in a baseball uniform with form-fitting light gray pants that showed off long, athletic legs. The text of his profile, however, mainly communicated a kind of berserk overexuberance. It overflowed with an extensive list of likes (sex, riding his bike, playing his guitar, smoking weed, "man smells," baseball, sex, cooking, swimming, sex, travel to France and Spain and Haiti and Italy, sex, drinking beer, sex, the park, sex) and dislikes ("Why are all you guys shaving off your body hair?!" he'd typed. "STOP! Be your NATURAL SELF!"), enough colorful emoji graphics to give the whole thing the look of a video game, and a head-spinning description of his professional life that began with the word *actor*, continued to *performer* and *writer* and *dancer*, and carried on at length, a half-dozen other half professions all tumbling over each other, signifying nothing but a powerful desire to be seen and heard. In spite of all that, the composite effect struck me as wholly positive and high-spirited. Real humanity must live behind, or maybe within, the calibrated self-presentation that marked these apps, I thought.

I hoped.

It was already late when Sam and I started texting. After a half hour of vague flirtation, he wrote *Come over* and *I want to meet you.* I protested at first—sleep sounded better. But after a bit more casual cajoling—*No pressure*, he wrote, *but I'm just hanging out, if you want to come hang out, we can chat and chill*—I caved. It would be almost one thirty in the morning by the time I got to his place, so I harbored few illusions about the nature of this "come hang out." While willing to accept the possibility of a simple, late-night neighborly social call between strangers, I assumed that barring various curveballs like imposterhood, repulsion, violence, murder, undisclosed extreme drug use, etc., one of us would be on top of the other before long.

That, of course, depended on nothing unfortunate happening on the way over. As I stepped out of my apartment, zipping my jacket up, I recalled a recent encounter with an older gay man— he had survived the AIDS crisis but had left New York haunted after seeing too many friends and intimates died—who had told me that, when he'd lived here in the 1970s and '80s, he would pretend he was severely, spastically retarded if he had to walk through a dodgy neighborhood by himself at night. We'd been at a dinner and he suddenly broke into an impression of himself pretending to be severely and spastically retarded—people of my generation generally no longer used the word *retarded*, but he did. The spectacle of this now returned to me, vivid in my mind's eye. It had surprised me at the time that someone who had seen so much death and suffering, felt so much loss, and lived with so many ghosts would reprise this act over dinner. I guess it had been a survival tactic. I would never know what it had been like to live in New York then, the depth of fear a person might feel on the streets at night, enough to make a person feign serious disability, act out a more manifest vulnerability. Still, I felt appalled. This man and I would have once been described, in once official medical language, as *deviants*, *inverts*. Then again, he had lived through a plague during which "our kind" was viewed as hateful, vile, diseased, degenerate, decadent, depraved. I hadn't: I only felt the radiation, saw the occasional nuclear shadow; the bomb had dropped, elsewhere, while I was chewing on a teething toy in my crib. I knew, too, that I was living out my own separate psychodrama: I often turned to older men looking for faultless and disciplined paragons of moral conduct and self-control. Unsurprisingly, I often felt disappointed. Who was to blame? A vision flashed: myself years later, an "older man," appalling in a new way, maybe even for what I was doing in my life at that moment, disappointing for the night I was about to have, a screen on which to project new shadow plays of failure.

The walk went fine. I'm large and male and bearded and I dress in a pretty unexciting way; people tend to leave me be.

Sam buzzed me into his building. He opened the door to his apartment on the third floor and welcomed me with a warm, hospitable air. "Welcome, handsome," he said. "Please, come in."

"Thanks."

"White boy walking in Flatbush after midnight. Good times." He made a noise of appreciation.

"You're sweet," I said. He wore a white tank top and basketball shorts. The front room of the apartment, which was also the living room, showed signs of a potentially sane individual. A bicycle hung from hooks on the ceiling. A record player in the corner, a few stacks of records. A French art deco poster decorated one wall. These encounters unfolded in such a cautious way, with one weighing potential danger and excitement in each passing moment, each detail, making split-second decisions about whether to stay or to flee. Sam, good-looking, his voice pleasant, gestured to the long couch. We took seats on opposite ends, both in casual, open postures.

"Nice place you have," I said, sincerely admiring it. I wanted nothing more than to live alone.

Sam thanked me. "I've lived here for almost ten years. Although I rent a room in Paris for part of the year. And then I have my place in Haiti."

Boastful, I thought. "In Haiti, huh?"

"My mom moved here from Haiti, so I have extended family there," he said. He was, meanwhile, looking me over with evident pleasure. "Plus real estate got pretty cheap after the earthquake, so I bought a little house."

"Interesting," I said. My hand brushed his arm by accident. I gave it a squeeze and smiled at him. I asked more questions and learned that he had been if not all of the professions listed in his profile then at least an actual actor/dancer. He had traveled the States as part of a fairly successful touring Broadway show. The conversation continued easily; he got us a couple of beers, expressing admiration for "anyone who can string together a sentence."

I was finding him charming and began to think I should go in for a move. Just then, though, a sound came from down the hall—things shuffled around, some movement.

"Sorry, just a moment," Sam said, getting up. "Someone else is here," he added as a kind of afterthought.

This gave me pause. Perhaps he had a roommate. He returned after a few moments, alone. "Do you live with someone?" I asked.

"No," he said, "a friend of mine is here." He sat back down. While I was trying to formulate the best way to ask *what kind of friend*, the friend emerged from the bedroom down the hall. A short-haired white guy in, I thought, his early forties, he too wore a tank top and shorts. He was muscular but also struck me immediately as dead-eyed, sex-haunted, the kind of muscle queen who spent an inordinate amount of time perfecting his body for the sport and pastime of sex.

These snap judgments came to me in a flurry even as I rose from the couch to shake his hand and introduce myself, feeling somehow that even in the midst of needing to recalibrate my understanding of the circumstances one ought to be polite. By the time we both sat down I'd formed a working impression of him as someone who had lost a significant portion of his life to hunting for sex. There was something ghostly about him, something not all there, as though a dogged nymphomania had thinned his spirit. He had cloaked himself in the visual symbols of gay male sexual athleticism with such determination—muscles, requisite tattoos, skimpy a-shirt—that whatever had been there before was now hard to discern. Though I prepared amid this storm of judgment to give him the benefit of the doubt, I already expected him to spoil everything.

Sam carried off this reveal of a second guest without comment. He simply continued, host-like, to engage me in curious conversation. Though he and I somehow went on talking like a couple of friendly neighbors, my attempts to integrate the sex-haunted muscle queen into our conversation failed repeatedly. A man of few words, he clearly expected something other than a chat in the living room; he was waiting for the other shoe, the sex shoe, to drop. And while I would have been happy to go to bed with Sam minutes earlier, this muscle queen bothered me, not only for his hollow gaze and air of sexual exhaustion but because he'd been sprung on me. Sam simply talked on, giving no indication at first that he cared one way or another whether the three of us had sex or not. He seemed perfectly willing to socialize at length while his spectral friend sat and stared at us.

The sensible thing to do at that point, given my hesitation, would've been to excuse myself. But being ambushed in this way brought out a kind of fighting, competitive instinct in me. What constituted the upper hand in such a situation? My most tried-and-true strategies remained journalistic. And so I took a breath, relaxed into my corner of the couch, and began to ask them an unceasing line of questions about their lives. I did this in as good-humored a way as possible, calling upon real curiosity mixed, at that moment, with discomfort. Dead-eyed muscle queen, where do you live? Where do you work? What is that work like for you? Who do you work with? What are they like? Where is your family? How well do they know you?

I thought this approach might irritate them and that I'd have to flee. Both Sam and his friend, though, responded to my questions and prompts with growing ease and openness; we talked for about an hour. The muscular one worked in fashion, at a company where he was one of the only men. "I've never felt so surrounded by women before," he said. Like a therapist, I tried to guide him toward unpacking this statement—*And how does that make you feel?*—but made little headway. "It's all very emotional," he said.

A tug-of-war soon began: every now and then Sam, dropping his host's mask, introduced a sexual subject or anecdote, trying to reroute the conversation. "The two of us were at a sex party recently," he said. "B—is my sex party buddy."

I responded with a nod, holding myself at a distance from the implied suggestion of group sex. Keen to keep them both talking, I asked an array of questions about how they had met, what the sex parties they went to were like, how one got invited to sex parties in the first place. ("Facebook," Sam said to this latter question.) Once they had talked about the logistics of sex parties at some length, I, having maintained an analytical remove up till then, said, "You know, it's not something that really interests me."

The atmosphere in the room changed: a little disappointment, frustration, offense. After all, I'd found a way to spend an entire hour preparing to suggest to them, indirectly, that I wasn't interested in having group sex that evening rather than clearly saying so upon the surprise appearance of the well-muscled man of fashion. And the truth was that the idea of group sex didn't bother me at all under the right circumstances. Group sex? Think of how much control you had to give up!

My approach that evening seemed to cast a spell of indirect-
ness over the room, for still no straightforward propositions
came forth. This, for instance, might have been the moment
for one of them to suggest that the night was over. However,
they both rose up to meet me in the talk game. After I gave
lip service for a short while to my preference for the intensity
of one-on-one connections, adding, for good measure, some
words about the deadening influence of too much sex, the ex-
cessive pressure and attention lavished upon sex among gay
men, and so on and so forth, the three of us segued into an
enjoyable stretch of recounting our own sexual histories, discussing our experiences with a range of activities, fetishes, et
cetera.

"My last experiment involved being flogged," said the dead-
eyed, haunted one, describing an encounter in San Francisco.
"Flogged by an older man."

"My mother once asked me why I loved white guys so much,"
said Sam. "I told her that it was because of the way they smelled.
When I said that, she wrinkled her nose and said, 'What, like a
wet potato chip?'"

We laughed together at this. Sam produced a tin of pepper-
mint Altoids. I took one in the heat of the moment, only realizing, once we all sat there in silence with Altoids in our mouths,
that to do so meant tipping the scales back in favor of group sex.
Why else freshen the breath?

During this lull—a lull for them, maybe, a contained panic
for me—Sam began talking about his neighbors, many of whom
he knew and occasionally cooked for. "You look too skinny," he
said, poking my arm and taking on a motherly tone. "You should
come over another night and I'll make you a home-cooked

meal." Mention of "another night" put me a bit more at ease; it meant, at the very least, that I probably wasn't going to get chopped into pieces or have my head cut off that evening. Then Sam began to tell a story about realizing one night that a woman from a neighboring building whom he knew vaguely from years of living there was being raped. She had, he said, a violent and unpredictable man in her life, a man who treated her poorly. He described this before casually mentioning that at the moment he realized the woman was being raped on the neighboring rooftop and calling for help, a sex party was taking place in his apartment. "So, four other guys were there," he said. "I keep a gun in the apartment," he added then, also casually, and proceeded to describe how he ran to his wardrobe to get the gun, returned to the very room we sat in at that moment, rallied the four men, and then, presumably with these half- or fully naked gay orgiasts in tow, climbed out the window and onto the roof, firing his gun into the air and shouting to the rapist that he had four men with him and that they would kill him if he didn't stop raping his neighbor.

I listened to this story in horrified amazement, meanwhile turning over the new and unsettling fact that Sam kept a gun in his apartment. On the one hand, Sam seemed to feel a need to have some surefire method of defense at hand in his neighborhood and evidently had a lot of strangers coming in and out of his apartment. On the other, the introduction of the gun into conversation had made me uneasy, for obvious Chekhovian reasons: the dramatic principle of "Chekhov's gun" insists that if a detail is introduced into a story, its "promise" must be fulfilled somehow. As Chekhov himself put it in a letter:

Remove everything that has no relevance to the story. If you say in the first chapter that there is a rifle hanging on the wall, in the second or third chapter it absolutely must go off. If it's not going to be fired, it shouldn't be hanging there.

I shouldn't be hanging here, I thought. I resolved to extract myself, but not until enough time had passed that my finally leaving would seem separate from the fact of the gun. We had already stretched our sublimating and tense game of denial on for an impressively long amount of time. Sam's friend, perhaps accepting at last that I intended to keep my clothes on, excused himself for a moment to do something in the bedroom—use his smartphone to find someone else, maybe. At this point I yawned—an actual, natural yawn, as it was now very late—and told Sam that I had enjoyed his company but should be going.

He shook his head. His eyes, deep brown, contained as many competing desires as his app profile did professions: kiss, slap, scold, read to the ground for wasting time, mother, feed, leave with, hold. "You be careful walking out of here at three in the morning, white boy," he said.

"I walked in just fine," I said.

Sam scratched his chin. "Well, that's true."

We stood near the doorway. Sam also looked apologetic. He repeated what seemed to be a sincere offer to cook for me, to see me under more relaxed circumstances. Then he said, under his breath: "I'm sorry."

I should have said I was sorry too. I should have said *forgive me*. Instead I laced my hiking boots, replying in a pleasant but noncommittal way, "For what?" When I stood, Sam pulled me against him, hugging me close. He pressed his face to my shoulder and inhaled deeply.

"Man," he whispered, "I love the way you smell."

"Like a wet potato chip," I said.

The muscle queen came back into the room. I walked over and shook his hand, said that it had been *a pleasure* to meet him and talk. He stared at me, done with whatever I seemed to think I was doing. "Yeah," he said.

"Good-bye," I said, addressing them both. And then, in a final gesture that surprised even me—it wasn't a gesture I'd ever really made before; not in this life, anyway—I pressed both my hands to my mouth and threw out a kiss, becoming an actress onstage at curtain call, an actress blowing kisses to her audience, having played, brilliantly, a man of *high moral character*. I backed out of the apartment.

A Sailor's Tale

I think often about a dish I cooked once, almost fifteen years ago, for a man sixteen years older than I, a man named John. I was twenty-one and had just started learning how to properly cook for myself. This was toward the beginning of a short-lived romantic career in Portland—the word *career* as descended from the Latin *carrus*, "chariot," calling to mind a Roman chariot speeding, careening. After several weeks of anxiously noting John's presence in our shared neighborhood coffee shop, I had worked up the nerve to ask this man—who was about as old as I am now—whether or not he would like to get together sometime. I forget exactly how I broke the ice. During that time spent nurturing the crush from afar, John, short and sturdy and with something like a permanent pout, would catch me glancing at him while I wrote at one table and he read the *Times* at another. He would look away, purse his lips, raise his dark eyebrows, and give his paper a good flap. This air of irritated, lordly disappointment deepened my resolve to serve him somehow once we actually got together properly. John would come to my house. Off, then, to scour the cookbooks at the Belmont Library, looking for a recipe.

Mission figs reconstituted in white wine, cooked with caramelized onions and herbs and served with goat cheese on crackers. The fig conjures fertility, lust, the abundant garden, plumpness and sweetness, a kind of classical Mediterranean enchantment. One could really reconstitute dried fruit in wine? I felt I had discovered a secret about the world—about a more beautiful survival—as the halved figs expanded in the pan, soaking up flavor, their shriveled skins becoming smooth again. (About figs, Hildegard of Bingen, the brilliant Benedictine abbess of the twelfth century, wrote in her *Physica*: "The fruit of this tree is not good for a person who is physically healthy to eat, since it affords him pleasure and gives him a swelled mind. . . . If a healthy person wishes to eat it, he should first soak it in wine or vinegar, so that its inconstancy is tempered. He should then eat it, but in moderation.") As John took the first bite he hummed with pleasure, declared *so good*. It was late spring. After eating, and before I invited him into my bedroom for the first time, we took a walk through Laurelhurst Park, circling the lake.

My biological father was a splendid cook. Or so says my mother. "He made a flourless chocolate cake to die for," she told me once, sipping a cup of black Constant Comment tea in her kitchen on Bainbridge Island. "I drew the line at garlic soup, though. Too much garlic." She liked to paint a picture of him growing up in a lively, multiethnic urban enclave in the Bronx, his Russian Jewish family arguing about cookery with the Hungarians, Italians, and Puerto Ricans they mixed with, slept with, married, loved. The two of them had met in Seattle, where he worked as a shoe salesman at Nordstrom. They split six years later when she decided to keep the baby. I'll never taste his cooking; during our one and only meeting, when I was seventeen, he told me that soda was poison, that drinking too much Coke had given him diabetes. He told me that he'd never stop smoking weed; he had offered to smoke me out and I'd said no, not because I didn't like smoking weed but because it seemed like he was acting out. A few days later he called to ask if he'd said anything to upset me (I think I mentioned earlier that he'd also told me my mother had tricked him into getting her pregnant—a brazen falsehood, she assured me). "No," I said. I never spoke to him again. Recently I found out that he'd died. It had taken two years from his death for me to find out, and I only found out because my mother was online scrolling through his sister's Facebook posts one afternoon. I was with a close friend when I found out. I cried for a little while and then, when he asked what I wanted to do, said, "I'd like to eat a steak at the Odeon." My mother wrote to ask for more details but the sister, who I'm told was once married to the actor who holds up baby Kunta Kinte at the beginning of the 1977 miniseries *Roots*, never replied. We still don't know what killed him. Time, I guess. My mother always maintained that he was one of "the great loves of her life."

What makes a love great?

The man in my life today has twenty-two years on me. When I mentioned this to a blunt Bosnian Serb woman a few years ago, a woman who, as a girl, had seen her best friend shot down in the street in Sarajevo—I was in Belgrade, dining on lamb chops and green salad in a restaurant where spouts in the ceiling occasionally released a light mist meant to cool the well-to-do patrons—she said to me, "So you need a father."

———

After the figs, I kept cooking for John. As often happens, I fixated on correcting a lack of knowledge, started photocopying pages from cookbooks at the library. Madhur Jaffrey's *World Vegetarian* got a good working over. (John eventually bought me a copy, which I threw out years later; he inscribed it in a way that later struck me as irritating. I only remember that it began, "Dear Evan: Now you'll never have to . . .") John enjoyed a lima bean stew with hot chili peppers and tomato and it became part of my regular rotation, along with Sri Lankan mustard greens with coconut and stuffed baby eggplant. I made a green Thai curry from scratch, hunting down lemongrass and a knob of galangal for the paste. The finished dish was so flavorful and fresh, the fragrance so tangy from the Kaffir lime leaves that I fell into raptures over my own success. Failures abounded, too, of course: fried sardines from *The Silver Spoon*, limp and bland from being frozen, too big and with too many little bones; things that took much longer to prepare than expected and left me frazzled and disappointed, left John and me both hungry and tired and unable to enjoy ourselves.

I sulked when things went wrong. As much as I admired John's mellifluous voice (deeper than mine, smooth, and with the faintest Georgian twang) and his strong, sure opinions, even those that grated on me (once, at a dinner I made for him and a few of my friends, he got into a heated argument with a young woman, a geologist, about Muslim women and the veil), as much as I wanted to drop to my knees before him, or to hold his lightly hairy legs apart and watch his eyes roll back as I pushed into him, leaned down to kiss him, John frightened me.

I didn't want to make any mistakes. Let me make one now: let me write a letter to him at a dining table in New York.

Dear John,

On one of our first dates, I left a bad tip at a diner on Belmont. You saw the tip and got pissed. "You can't do that," you said. On our way out, walking down the sunny, tree-lined streets, you berated me: "I can't believe you would do that. What if I hadn't noticed? If I only found out later that you'd left that tip, I wouldn't be able to show my face in that place again." You showed your face to me, handsome and scowling: you could be an angry teacher. I knew so little about the world then. I didn't know, for instance, how to tip correctly. You fumed, storming down the street. Maybe I apologized or got defensive; I undoubtedly fell silent before long, ashamed.

Were you angry that I knew so little? That I longed for you to teach me?

I hated your anger then. Your anger filled me with fury, with fear that you would leave me. When you went out riding your bike at night, disappearing for hours at a time, I feared you might be cheating on me in video booths or parks. Never said anything. Felt crazy. It embarrasses me now to look back and see myself so stiff with tension, sitting by your side on the porch when you returned, panting and sweaty, to curl up in my arms. I could barely take a breath; nightmares ate my mind.

I think I wanted you to leave me. I think it might have turned me on. A burning fear confirmed.

Never said anything. I hoped I'd learn, watching you, what life is—what it means to be here. To be, of all things, a man. Did you like it a little, my being afraid? Did it turn you on a little, too? A lot? Maybe you never really noticed; it just charged the air around us. Maybe my silence frightened you. What man, knowing himself, could fail to fear another?

It would be years before I learned to cop to not knowing, to terrors both cosmic and intimate. Years more before I saw that all men fear. I'm learning now: no great love is fearless. I'm learning: fear points many ways forward, down forking paths.

I remember something you said to me one day, after I'd been fixing new recipes for over a year. "I thought it was exciting when you started teaching yourself how to cook," you said, sitting in the emerald green armchair in your living room, drinking black tea from a rough ceramic mug, "but now you've really gotten good, and I'm starting to feel intimidated."

Were you afraid that if I learned to cook too well—to care that much more for myself, to transform my character through work, through skill—that I'd leave you?

Well, Dear John,

I left you.

Evan

———

During our first trip to England together—my first trip there, period—my partner tells the anecdote about how we met.

"I met him at the bookstore," he says, addressing three people who've invited us for a meal. He grins. We're sitting by a warm fireplace in a pub just outside town in Oxford, England, a charming stone building situated on a stretch of the Thames and with the Port Meadow just beyond. Green grass and bright yellow buttercups cover the Port Meadow this time of year. Out there, too, rise round barrows—long mounds of earth where people buried their dead more than two thousand years ago. The pub itself has been here for eight hundred years, although the current building has only been standing about half that time. It's also said to be haunted by a sailor who, heartbroken at the hands of someone lost to time, drowned himself at a "well-known suicide spot" nearby. His spirit returns to drink his sorrows away, endlessly circling back to this place.

Five of us sit in a U shape around a table before the fire. My partner continues: "I thought he seemed like a friendly person. Tall and calm. So I was sitting there on the chair, and meanwhile he's walking around the shop, shelving books and so on."

I pick at some fish cakes made with rainbow trout and sorrel, drink from a glass of English cider. For about ten or fifteen minutes, I'd enjoyed a solid lead against my friend in a game of checkers. But then I'd lost my focus and made two really boneheaded moves in a row. My friend shakes his head now as he carries on thinning the ranks of my infantry.

"We started chatting about some book—*The Blue Flower*, Penelope Fitzgerald," my partner says. "And he came over and stood by me. But then he took a step away from me as we were talking. He planted himself at a greater distance."

On the couch, my partner imitates me holding myself at a distance from him. Smiling, I look down at the formations on the checkerboard. We've moved from familiar constellations there to teeming chaos. My partner pauses to take a bite of his roasted sea bream. "And so I said to him, with the other bookstore people standing there too: 'Are you afraid of me?'"

Our eyes meet. Warmth. I make another move that feels strategic at first, but immediately reveals itself as the height of folly.

"He looked at me for a minute, calm as can be," he continues, "and then said, very cheerfully, 'A little!'"

The five of us share a laugh, our bodies shaking merrily as the wind blows the willows outside the old pub in Oxfordshire. "I thought that would be a good place to begin," I say, and then proceed to lose, and lose, and lose, until only one perfectly round, ridged black checker stares back at me from the board, gleaming in the warm light of the fire, facing death in every direction.

First Date

Theo had a handsome face. The word *devilish* came to mind; he had this kind of satanic goatee. He talked a lot, bridging any threatening chasm of silence with chatter. We were sitting in a bar in Park Slope, on a first date in 2015. He really let loose when the conversation turned to family, going to competitive lengths to establish the dysfunction run rampant among his kin. His sister, he said, had been the golden child for years. A high-achieving, straight-A student, a polished and successful postcollege professional. Then she'd had a complete fucking breakdown from the stress of maintaining a perfect image. "She moved back in with my parents, until they asked her to leave," he said. "She'd become totally unmanageable. She attacked me one Christmas. She just flew at me. Started hitting me, calling me an asshole. We hid all the booze, so she put hand sanitizer up her ass to try and get alcohol into her body." She'd since called him often, asking for money.

I went to the bar for another beer. When I returned, the dark running gag we'd established over text days earlier reared its head, the one about my being a potential sex app serial killer. A troubled look crossed Theo's face. "I'm sorry," I said. "I watch too many crime shows."

"Yeah," he said. "I have trouble with those."

"Too scary?"

"It's not that," he said. He cleared his throat. "A friend of mine in high school, in Virginia, was kidnapped and killed by a serial murderer."

My hand flew to my mouth. I wanted to stuff back inside of it everything I'd already said in a boundary-free fit of imaginative play and improv about being a killer. I apologized.

"It was a long time ago," he assured me. He said he'd come to terms with the killing of his friend and her sister as best he could.

"We don't have to talk about this if you don't want to," I said, "but do you mind if I ask what happened?"

Theo smiled. "So you can write about it later?" Then he shrugged. "No, that's fine, whatever." His friend and her sister, one a teenager, the other a few years younger, had been abducted by the killer—later described as a "sexually sadistic psychopath"—outside their house. Their bodies had turned up in a river in central Virginia not long after. Had the police ever found him? "It took five or six years." I'd later learn that Richard Evonitz had finally been identified when one of his victims escaped after being kidnapped and raped and called the police. They pursued him to Sarasota, Florida, in a high-speed chase until, surrounded, he shot himself. "When they found his car," said Theo, "my friend's fingerprints were still in the trunk."

I could only shake my head, disgusted by the injustice of such a death. "It's long in the past," he said, "but now you see why I have trouble with those crime shows." The atrocious acts of Evonitz hung over our conversation now. I sat with my guilt at having touched upon a sensitive subject by way of reckless play.

Theo excused himself to use the restroom. While he was gone, my thoughts wandered. I swirled the last of the brown-black beer at the bottom of my glass. I wondered what my mother might make of the deaths of those young sisters in central Virginia. I recalled having an argument with her when I was younger. We were driving along a curving, heavily tree-lined two-lane high-way to Port Angeles. A family, we'd both heard, had been killed while driving along that same stretch at night. A trucker coming the opposite direction had fallen asleep at the wheel, something like that. The children had been sleeping in the backseat, she told me. Although now that I think of it, no one could know such a thing; a compulsion to dramatize. Maybe the compulsion to dramatize is *mine* and she never actually said that. In any case, as a way of maybe putting me or herself at ease, she concluded of this family's death, "It was their time."

I seethed in the passenger seat. "How can you say that?" I said. "How can you imply that everyone dies when they're supposed to?" I was barely twenty at the time—in fact, it would've been early summer, just weeks before Richard Evonitz shot himself. I wondered now how the suite of hopeful ideas my mother lived by—a prearranged path in life, a benevolent and conspiring Uni-verse, those various Laws of Attraction, meaningful and timely death, reincarnation—would apply to Theo's friend and her sis-ter and their sexually sadistic psychopathic killer. Presumably all three of them would have, by way of the transmigration of souls, returned by now, carrying with them the trace of those lives that came to heinous ends around the turn of the new century. Did souls travel in families? In packs? In troupes, like those old itin-erant playing companies? Did they hunt each other? I thought again of that conversation with my mother about past lives, the one when she handed me a copy of that photograph, printed off the Internet, of Lady Duff Twysden, her buddy Ernest Hemingway, and four others seated at a café table in Pamplona, and said to me, "Do you see it? It's in the eyes." What else, I wondered, downing the last of a bitter beer, could one see in the eyes? What else lived in the eyes—what else that had lived before?

When Theo returned, I was quiet. I lifted my head to look at him, met his gaze as he sat down smiling. It had a shimmer in it, a lively light dancing in irises the color of chestnut, filling the black pupils with hungry life. "So," he said. "How are you getting home?"

I had to laugh.

Persuasion

A few years ago I was working in another New York bookstore, Three Lives & Company, making about fourteen dollars an hour while writing on the side, when someone I recognized walked through the door: a man likely to be in his fifties and for whom I had worked about fifteen years earlier. I hadn't seen him in all that time. I had been an intern at a magazine in Portland, Oregon—one of five internships I did in a half-baked, confused, uncertain effort to find a job in editorial or journalism—and this guy, Russ, had worked as an editor there at the time. Though one runs into people in this way more often as the years go by, for some reason I felt particularly flabbergasted by the encounter. It came home to me while I stood there chatting with him from my side of the counter, ringing up his books and running his credit card, just how long I'd been trying to carve out a life for myself as a writer, just how many internships, odd jobs, loans, relocations, classes, seminars, and gambles had filled the last fifteen years. *Gamble* began, more and more, to feel like the operative word. (In fact, I've just decided that the alternative title for this collection is *The Gambler*.) What also came back, a flash in my mind, was an email Russ had written to me. I'd written to him a couple of years after my internship—after ignoring the sound professional advice of one of the other editors: that if I really wanted to make my way as a journalist, I should consider moving to a small town and throwing myself into covering the local beat, so that I could build up my competence properly—written him an email saying that I was thinking of going into advertising but felt torn between the glossy comforts it supposedly offered and a more uncertain path toward writing fiction. (This was not the first time I'd felt torn between a path with more certainty in it and that of writing fiction. When I took a meeting with one of my first college professors, an ethnomusicologist, because I wanted to know more about the field she worked in, she became very excited, working hard to sell me on a career like her own. Faced with the "But what about writing?" question, she said, "Writing is easy. All you need is one good idea and a computer.") He wrote a short email back to me—we weren't in the habit of corresponding and I'd never before turned to him for professional or life advice—saying, "I don't know what siren song has caught your ear," something to that effect, "but you're a good writer."

People generally don't need that much encouragement. As I stood there in the bookstore scraping by, I began to recall the siren song in some detail. I was living in Portland in the mid-2000s. I lived in a big Victorian house on Belmont with three other people. My rent was just over three hundred dollars a month. While freelancing for a newsweekly, I picked up some lucrative copywriting work through someone on the business side of *Portland Monthly*. She set up a meeting between me and the head of marketing for a master-planned suburban community in Beaverton. I took the light rail out to his office, where he told me about the project: a brochure that advertised the mixed-use residential-commercial spaces to potential buyers.

"It needs to be *hip-hop*," he said, referring to the tone he hoped the brochure would strike. "You know: champagne, hot tubs." In my memory he has dark, gelled hair, skin made paler and more sallow by long, stressful hours indoors working in the marketing department, a red tie. I couldn't believe the words *hip-hop* had come out of his mouth in reference to a master-planned suburban housing community, but then again, hip-hop and rap had taken hold as the dominant cultural product marketed to kids like me and my friends when we were teens and preteens on Bainbridge Island, described by *Vogue* in recent years as the "West Coast equivalent of Nantucket." Once, when my mother was going through a hard time with her own mother, my brother, who was maybe fifteen at the time and whose father (we had different fathers) had been interned at the Tule Lake camp for Japanese-Americans as a boy, said to her, "Mom, you need to tell that bitch to step off."

So: hip-hop it would be. What he meant, I knew, was that I should write the copy in a way that made young middle-class professionals feel as though they had disposable income to burn, that their lifestyles were glittering and glamorous. The likelihood that almost everyone who ended up living in that master-planned community would be white seemed pretty high to me, but that was a concern for another day. When the head of marketing asked me how much money I charged for my brochure-writing services, I quoted him an estimate that felt obscene coming out of my mouth but that had been recommended to me by a then-current book about freelancing. Though I would have to take taxes out myself, it was still about seven times as much per hour as I was making fifteen years later at the bookstore when Russ walked in.

The marketing guy nodded. "That seems low," he said, adding for my instruction that "most guys" charged him an hourly rate closer to ten times the amount I was making fifteen years later at the bookstore. I knew then that there might be something to this copywriting thing.

———

The brochure work took a decent amount of effort, but the fact that I could do it from home made me feel like I'd beat the system somehow. That a private courier both delivered work to me and carried away my completed work made me feel like a prince. I began, of course, to imagine all of the worldly wonders to which this line of work might lead: living alone in my own apartment, say, or traveling the world, or buying clothes that fit me—the same things I now catch myself fantasizing that writing novels and essays while teaching might one day afford me. *Hip-hop.* At the time I had checked a book out of the library called *The Well-Fed Writer*—a guide written by a professional freelance copywriter about how to build up and sustain an independent business, promising that, if one chose, one could work full-time from home and earn a six-figure salary. I was used to working various service and labor jobs while pursuing unpaid internships; six figures seemed to me like something that only extremely powerful people in New York made, people who occupied a rarefied sphere of life. I imagined them gliding from the doors of glass office towers into gleaming black cars that ferried them seamlessly between lunch meetings with powerful clients, everyone dining on pheasant and aspic while they discussed magazine layouts. At twenty-one I had very little sense of how a professional life developed; jobs with six-figure salaries seemed to me like something you lucked into by some astonishing stroke of good fortune, by being in the right place at the right time. In fact, it would be many years before I met people my own age who, I came to understand, had actually planned on walking into a particular career immediately after college and who *expected* to earn six-figure salaries at some point in their lives, just as one might expect one's hair to eventually start thinning—a fact of life.

In any case, I mention these fantasies because, as had happened before and would happen again, they briefly derailed me, distracting me from the realities of work with slick promises of lifestyle. In the small city of Portland, the glittering inner circle in this regard, the looming ideal, was the independent advertising agency Wieden+Kennedy. I first became aware of their existence shortly after moving there, as their reach overlapped the hipster alt-weekly circles I moved in. They were a prestige institution that appeared to employ the best and brightest of the apparently shiftless young creative set while also compensating them handsomely. Though some of my friends, acquaintances, and lovers scoffed at this ultimately corrupt and capitalistic enterprise disguised in a cool-hunter's motley rags, I fell under the spell of its aloof and self-satisfied exclusivity. It looked fresh and lively from the outside. I'd always associated working in advertising with a kind of tired, middle-aged office life and felt surprised at the time that it could dress like me, talk like me, listen to my music, read my books, wear a face like mine. They'd made their name, their fortune, and their reputation by establishing Nike— one of the brands most often vilified, pilloried, and taken to task for unethical labor practices in the pages of *Adbusters* and elsewhere—and suddenly it seemed dazzling and fantastic to me that there was a place where creativity and play came together with cool, colorful athletic streetwear, and where those who supplied the former could gain access to all the money associated with the latter. I thought of their offices as a kind of temple. I'd heard they were modern and chic, designed by a visionary architect.

With this in mind I tried to find an internship at an ad agency. Having no background, specialized knowledge, or actual passion for the work itself or its history—it was the spell that held sway then, the vision of being a well-compensated, stylish "creative" (it was around this time that I first heard that word used as a noun)—I was turned away from all of the major commercial agencies in town and wound up at one that specialized in business-to-business advertising. That meant creating ads for clients like Freightliner Trucks, ads to be placed in trade magazines targeted at the trucking industry and more specifically at people in a position to make decisions about what kinds of trucks to buy for a trucking fleet. My supervisors were two *creatives*: middle-aged copywriter guys with beer guts more in keeping with how I'd imagined advertising before learning about Wieden+Kennedy.

"I'm sorry we don't really have a proper place to put you," said the senior creative, twisting his mouth. "But we've set up a temporary intern's desk for you in the hallway."

In the middle of the office there was a kind of dark corridor, a hallway that led to a supply closet of some kind. There they had set up a long desk with an old computer. I was enthusiastic about it; I was grateful to be taken on as an intern in the first place, since it must have meant they saw some potential in me, some possibility. That, I figured, might one day lead me straight to an office in the glassy, light-filled, airy temple of Wieden+Kennedy or some similarly fresh-faced, trend-conscious agency.

Though I jumped at any opportunity to learn what I thought I wanted to know, it didn't take long for me to discover—or half-discover, let's say—that the day-to-day work of an adman at a business-to-business agency—working on a request for a proposal for a company that sold mechanical parts of some kind, etc., etc.—held little intrinsic interest for me. It was the supposed glamour, the siren song, that had really taken hold. It's difficult for me to recall what was going through my mind at that time. On the one hand, in my twenties I enjoyed a simple curiosity about most situations, and the sense of endless possibility I felt during those years meant that no variety of work felt like a waste of time or life-force; it seemed advantageous to have as wide a range of experiences as possible on the way to zeroing in on my true calling. On the other, an overly open and impressionable nature coupled with contradictory cravings for structure and chaotic freedom meant that I could be, let's say, both an attractive candidate and a risky investment under the best of circumstances. What I do know about that era of my life was that I was liable to throw myself into things with the utmost initial enthusiasm only to turn back and flee when the going got tough. There's no great story there: I was immature. I was also a pretty easy mark, all things considered. Had I come of age in the 1960s, I probably would have ended up joining one or more cults or intentional communities, leaving them when they got too weird and talking about them as a subject in a documentary a few decades later. Had a recruitment officer for the State Department found me during my college years and put even a little effort into flattering me for my evident but ill-developed talent for languages, I likely would've done whatever he or she told me to do, including joining a branch of the armed forces. As it was, the quest for a quick and easy outward appearance of "creativity" guided a lot of my decisions at the time.

Not all of them, but a lot of the work-related ones. At the same time, I was seeing an older man (the *Dear John* of that earlier essay), contending with a meeting of strong personalities, learning more about sex and relationships and communications and my own good qualities and flaws. We'd been seeing each other for about a year. He would sometimes become exasperated by my tendency to overextend myself in my quest to try everything, to be everything. I remember meeting up with him on a bench overlooking Mount Tabor Park around that time. In addition to my internship at the ad agency and my regular freelancing, I'd taken a part-time job working at a warehouse where I helped distress lighting fixtures made in China and India to make them look like American antiques. I would sit for hours rubbing doorknobs with steel wool or lowering things into different chemical baths. "You have two jobs on top of your writing," he said. "When am I ever going to see you?"

He was suspicious, too, of the ad world in general, especially the inner circle allure Wieden+Kennedy held for me. It's funny now to think that a place like that, in an industry like that, could have captivated my fascination so powerfully, but I was looking for a place where I felt like I belonged. When Wieden+Kennedy later put out an open call for a kind of elite year-long program— W+K 12, which was something like an internship, apprenticeship, creative incubator, or educational program, but also a moneymaking and talent-grabbing scheme; the twelve people selected had to pay the agency to participate—I eagerly applied, sending in a portfolio of my journalism clips. "I would do it if it works out," I said to John. "I would pay. It's worth it." Who was I trying to convince? He wasn't easily persuaded, anyway; he viewed the whole pursuit with understandable suspicion. The supposed secrets of that inner ring called out to me, seductive. I hadn't yet encountered a speech by C. S. Lewis called "The Inner Ring," the message of which I returned to again and again over the years as a way of keeping myself on course:

> The quest of the Inner Ring will break your hearts unless you break it. But if you break it, a surprising result will follow. If in your working hours you make the work your end, you will presently find yourself all unawares inside the only circle in your profession that really matters. You will be one of the sound craftsmen, and other sound craftsmen will know it. This group of craftsmen will by no means coincide with the Inner Ring or the Important People or the People in the Know. It will not shape that professional policy or work up that professional influence which fights for the profession as a whole against the public: nor will it lead to those periodic scandals and crises which the Inner Ring produces. But it will do those things which that profession exists to do and will in the long run be responsible for all the respect which that profession in fact enjoys and which the speeches and advertisements cannot maintain.

It's funny: a novelist I knew back then—someone whom I tried in various subtle ways to conscript as a mentor but who never quite responded to my advances—had done some occasional contract work for Wieden+Kennedy. Confronted with the question of lending his services to the advertising industry, he described it to me as "working for the church," the same way painters during the Renaissance, for example, accepted commissions to paint frescoes or create sculptures inside cathedrals. I admired the realism of that characterization and held that ideal in mind. At the same time I envied the way that he could so casually pick up a gig here and there doing some kind of one-off project for a prestigious institution. That kind of freedom to pick and choose amazed me—could a person really live and work that way?

When the mind behind W+K 12, a creative named Jelly Helm—he had given himself that first name, or else it was a creative shortening of some kind; in any case it's clear that it was meant to connote something creative and unique and gelatinous—invited me to participate as a potential candidate in a kind of day-long group interview process at the agency, a combination of one-on-one talks, improv games, and other various and sundry creative encounters, it felt like a heavenly ray of light had broken through a dark sky, like the way forward toward my fate was opening up and a voice from the clouds was coaxing me on. I felt giddy with anticipation. At the very least, I would finally get a tour of the temple.

The day came, and Jelly, tall with dark, wavy hair and a somewhat eccentric general demeanor that seemed slightly studied to me, guided the twenty-four-odd candidates through the offices, breaking us into groups for presentations and activities. He spoke to us of his interest in improv, of the book *Impro* by Keith Johnstone (which, legitimately curious, I later read; it's amazing), and we participated in exercises with an improv expert on the agency's private indoor basketball court. We met with different people in the agency—art directors, copywriters, buyers, account managers—who told us about their jobs. Jelly made impassioned, confident claims about creativity that captivated me, adding at one point, to demonstrate the results of his own conversion experience to true creativity, that he used to admire the Beatles but now believed that Yoko Ono was more creative and interesting than any of them. A little more than halfway through the day, Jelly surprised us with what is some people's greatest fear. He gathered us in a small room where we heard the murmur of a crowd beyond one door. We were all, he explained, to give a short, impromptu speech of some kind to the whole agency, which was gathered beyond the door on the tiered steps of an amphitheater in the center of the open-plan building.

There was a certain heady subversiveness to it all—none of this seemed like the kind of thing that happened in a workplace. To be thrown into different challenges and asked to improvise from moment to moment excited me. I wasn't that intimidated by public speaking, anyway. I don't recall much about my own speech, though I do remember an embarrassing moment where, in hindsight, I resorted to a trick to take the attention off me: I talked about the other candidates. As I'd chatted with them throughout the day and observed them going through the same tasks and encounters, their apparent savvy and self-assurance impressed me. All of them seemed to have more direction in their lives than I did, though it was easy to imagine, back then, that everyone else knew what they were doing while I wandered, lost, from thing to thing, doing my best to muster up new displays of zeal and charm, the kind of dance that might persuade someone to buy you, to love you, to take you in. So, after saying whatever it was I said about myself, I half-turned to the waiting group and said into the microphone, "Seriously, though, I would marry every one of you," a bid for laughter and a desperate attempt to escape being further scrutinized. Further scrutiny might mean, after all, that people could see I didn't belong there or, in fact, anywhere. Further scrutiny might mean being banished into the wilderness. I got a fine amount of applause.

The most difficult test over, we were then cut loose to eat sandwiches with brie, green apples, and hot mustard—even the food seemed unusual and creative!—and to chat with people at the agency while we waited to be summoned into a room for our final interview with Jelly.

I ended up standing and talking with a woman, another creative, maybe in her late twenties or early thirties, on the steps of the auditorium. After some initial chitchat, she wanted to know what ads I liked. "What campaigns are you interested in?" she asked.

I squirmed, faced for the first time that day with an actual question about advertising. "Apple," I said. I had bought an iMac laptop not long before that—swayed, no doubt, by the cool image the company had cultivated, so it was the first thing that came to mind.

The woman nodded approvingly. "That's a great one," she said. "They just *work*." She was referring to the vision of the computers that the ads sold. I remembered reading something that either Dan Wieden or David Kennedy had said about the strongest brands being, essentially, associated with strong, simple verbs—they had managed that with Nike, with their signature slogan, "Just Do It." (Funny, but as I write this I can't recall whether or not we met either Wieden or Kennedy that day.) Somehow I hadn't thought about what she was saying before: the ads for Apple products had distinguished themselves in the computer market in part because they dispensed with trying to explain anything about the actual technology of personal computers or MP3 players, especially how they worked, instead riding on the great insight that the average consumer actually didn't want to think about those things. The ads sent a message of ease of use, products for everyone that required no specialized knowledge. They just worked, these computers. And didn't you want to have at least one thing in your life that just *worked*?

Soon Jelly found me and asked if I was ready to sit down and chat with him. We went into a private meeting room (in my memory it's glass on all sides, the kind of transparent room in the middle of an open plan that people passing by could look into). The first thing that Jelly asked me, in his endlessly adaptive, friendly way, was about the moment in my speech when I drew attention away from myself, putting the spotlight on the others. "That was a nice thing to say," he said. "What made you do that?"

I stammered through some kind of explanation about how fascinating and interesting everyone was whom I'd met that day, how I wanted to show my appreciation, acknowledge all that talent.

Jelly nodded and smiled, sticking his lower lip out, vaguely sagelike. He didn't pursue that line of questioning further but seemed to be listening very closely, absorbing secret meanings behind my utterances that I was perhaps years from comprehending. He started flipping through the portfolio I'd sent in.

"You're really prolific!" he said. "You've written so much over the last couple of years. I was really impressed. How do you manage it?"

That was a more comfortable topic for me. I began to talk about a book I'd picked up when I first started freelancing for the alt-weekly, a book called *Writing on Both Sides of the Brain,* by Henriette Klauser. Klauser taught me to start separating the drafting process and revision; my productivity improved once I learned to negotiate with my "Inner Critic"—that voice that stops you from starting, that nitpicks when you're writing poorly, that interferes with your getting the raw material on the page. Plus, I added, I had asked the paper to throw any assignment they had at me; I would write about food, movies, books, music, anything. Deadlines helped. It was all a great way to get practice. My aim had just been to write and publish as many pieces as possible, I said. What I was writing about didn't matter.

Jelly liked that. "That's great about the Inner Critic," he said. "It's so important to work on that. It can free up so much creativity."

I felt the tides turning in my favor; a spot among the final thirteen seemed within my reach. Our exchange about the Inner Critic made me feel as though I actually knew a thing or two about the pragmatic creative process. Might that very knowledge be my key to the inner ring?

Everything changed in the next minute. I don't even remember what question Jelly asked. It must have been something like, *Why are you here?* or *What brings you to Wieden+Kennedy? What made you apply for this program in the first place?*

I'm not sure what happened to me in that moment. Something came out of my mouth that I had no intention of saying. I had never imagined myself saying it and had never said it before in my life. The day had been full of responsive improvisation, so maybe that had primed me somehow—maybe I simply said the first thing that came to mind, in keeping with what I perceived to be the rules of the game that Jelly had laid out for us. That, though, begs the question of why it was the first thing that came to my mind. Where did it come from? I didn't think; I simply spoke, and when I spoke it was as though some other power spoke through me, someone other than the person who had spent that whole day and the weeks leading up to it jumping through improvisational hoops, trembling in a kind of giddy anxiety about the promises of the agency's creative lifestyle. Even as the words came out of my mouth I wondered where they came from. What I said, sitting across from Jelly Helm in a small private meeting room in the prestigious ad agency that had helped establish Nike as a globally successful brand, was this: "I'm on a spiritual journey."

Jelly's eyes widened. He looked surprised. He smiled, but he also looked away from me for a second as he said, "Right on, man," perhaps recalculating his sense of who was sitting across from him in that glassy office. I felt it in the air: a recalibration, perhaps involuntary—in any case, perfectly understandable—of how sane I was. Jelly, though, didn't miss a beat—he hadn't missed a beat all day. He really had learned some powerful techniques and maneuvers from all his studies of creativity. He had, all along, the air of someone who had once been something completely different than what he had become, someone who had transformed himself. Quickly zeroing in on this new tack in the conversation, he asked me the question, only natural, "And where has it taken you?"

I hadn't thought about that before. In fact, I hadn't known, until those words came unexpectedly tumbling out of my mouth, that I even *was* on a spiritual journey. I still look back on that moment with unsatisfied curiosity, unsure of its meaning. Deeper truth? Self-sabotage? Ill-considered improvisational move? Desperate attempt, in the face of gnawing feelings of insufficiency and fraudulence, to impart an aura of divine importance and purpose to my being there? Misguided, resentful lashing out at a male authority figure? Predestination?

Some partial truth: if I'd made the final cut after telling Jelly Helm that I was on a spiritual journey, I probably still *would* have paid to spend a year working in the agency's creative incubator. The moment was not a revelatory conversion experience, though it's stayed with me to this day. I didn't walk out of the offices of Wieden+Kennedy thinking that the angel of pure creativity had swooped down and guided me away from the corrupting influence of advertising; I still admire people who make great ads and have no doubt that there is plenty of nobility, personal integrity, philosophical searching, true creativity, admirable practical competence, and sound, respectable craft in advertising, alongside what can be found in any industry: all that which is rotten, evil, lost, false, what C. S. Lewis called "scoundrelism." I can say that in the days and weeks after I received my rejection letter, the allure of the agency faded somewhat until I found myself no longer in the first flush of enchantment, aware of the extent to which I had simply been dazzled. I didn't want it enough to keep trying.

Before I got to that point, however, I fumbled for a response to Jelly's question. *Where has it taken you?* God knows where I thought I was going in those days; confronted with the question,

I couldn't even articulate where I was. I groped in my mind for an answer until I found the only word that seemed right, seemed true.

I spread my arms out wide, turning my head back and forth as I gazed through the glass walls and out at the agency, where real work was taking place all around us. I did this as if to point out something essential that Jelly had been overlooking all along—as if to point out some breathtaking, fundamental truth about life. "Here," I said. "It's brought me here."

Vanishing Days

I walked by the bathhouse building several times. It had a discreet entrance, a nondescript façade. On the few past occasions when I'd gone into a bathhouse—in gay old Barcelona, for instance, where, you'll recall, I almost took a job in one—it had been this way: a last-minute mental fencing match, a wrestling with the bathhouse angel, *Thinking Fast and Slow About Whether or Not to Enter the Bathhouse*. Now I was in gay old Montreal, passing along Saint-Catherine Street again. I turned a corner, walking in an expanding spiral away from the bathhouse on the Plateau, then reversed my course, spiraling back toward it. This prolonged drama of indecision might, I thought, either exhaust my racing mind, which was eminently capable of talking me out of doing anything ever, or successfully muzzle that sweaty, stinking animal curiosity that had gotten me moving in the first place. I was kidding myself: during that part of my life, curiosity won out almost every time, at least when it came to the question of entering some gay lair or another. I craved a connection—higher, lower, however one came by it—and the craving mastered me.

A thunderstorm had passed through earlier in the day. Now, however, as I made my way back to Saint-Catherine, the sky was "clear," which is to say: oceanic, dark, deep inasmuch as it stretched out and out into the great, grave beyond. I knew almost no one in town and I'd be leaving soon. Straight couples and small groups strolled along the park, speaking Québécois French, West African French, English, blends of these, other tongues. Soon the dotted, solemn yellow-white lights of the park gave way to the cheerful ones of the boulevard, where people dined and drank *en plein air* or in luminous rooms behind glass. A pleasing aroma of flesh and char and fat wafted from a brightly lit kebab shop.

I entered the bathhouse. Indigo bulbs gave the antechamber a warm glow. No attendant appeared to be on duty, just a nerve-racking absence at the front counter. Keys on coiled red rubber bands hung from hooks on the wall. The ideal me wouldn't need to wait, standing there with his want exposed. He'd know in his stride all the laws of movement between one world and the other. In fact, the ideal me wouldn't even be an individual, differentiated body: the essential crisis, the cosmic crisis then driving my life, was a rampant desire to feel at home everywhere, to absorb and master all codes, all languages—from hieroglyphics to the hanky code to HTML—to devour everything and be devoured by everything and so become one with the world, never again so youthfully lost, so stiff with insecurity. A little relief from being human, or maybe a lot. Was that too much to ask?

Just when I feared I'd have to call into the bathhouse in order to soldier on toward this goal, an unsmiling, sinewy man swept in behind the counter, running a hand through his messy black hair.

"*Bonsoir*," he said. He appraised me with a certain flatness of manner, a tired eye.

A short exchange in French followed. Once I paid, the attendant switched to English. "Come this way," he said. He opened a door into a second antechamber. There were a few plush-looking chairs. A man in his forties or fifties sat on one. (He'd probably been chatting with the attendant when I arrived, but what about?) At the far end of the room was a bar, unmanned. The attendant must have usually covered that, too, flitting from one task to the next, head skeleton of the bathhouse skeleton crew.

With a tight-lipped, thin smile, head skeleton handed me a towel and key. "You are room number nineteen," he said. A comforting reduction: I was a room now. He gestured down a dark corridor, nodded, told me to *have fun*, then returned to sit with his friend, who was watching me.

The halls seemed deserted. Many neighboring rooms waited, empty, open. I found number 19 and closed the door behind me. It had a hard little bench and a tall locker. I undressed, folded my clothes neatly, and put them all away.

———

Questionable thinking had brought me to Montreal in the first place. I'd been laid off from that job answering phones at the San Francisco Ballet, the one where I'd sold all those *Nutcracker* tickets and fielded calls from patrons of the arts who feared contracting tuberculosis, and so decided to celebrate joblessness by leaving the country. A friend deposited my unemployment checks for me while I was in Canada. At that time I was also infatuated with a drag queen who'd been sober for many years; the solid sense of identity he seemed to find between performance and sobriety fascinated me. So what if he had an irritating nickname for me ("The English Patient"—I couldn't keep weight on, I was disappearing), so what if he criticized my coffee-stained teeth even though his were crooked, so what if he felt contempt and fear and incredulity in the face of my desire for him. *So what?* In some hidden chamber of myself I nurtured a hunch that taking shelter in intimacy could really roughly approximate the relief I'd found a handful of times in things like smoking heroin, before the ex who introduced me to that, as you'll also recall, died from his addiction: relief from being human, from being a frightened, feeling animal. And though I told myself I'd joined AA shortly after meeting the drag queen because of a preexisting yen for substances of all kinds, the truth is that I longed to absorb any and all details related to his life. I wanted his life in my veins; too much of my own there. I'd failed to properly work the first of the twelve steps ("Admit you are powerless over alcohol") by the time I left for Quebec, but continued my performance of sobriety for most of the trip—until, released from my obsession with a man I'd watched put on pantyhose and Kryolan makeup to lip-sync Tina Turner and Björk and Siouxsie Sioux on the stages of small, booze-soaked gay bars, I finally ordered a glass of pinot grigio on the terrace of a bistro during my last week in Canada and drank it alone. I recall wishing the wine would have some sublime effect on me—I'd held off drinking, after all, for months. But I only felt like I'd had a glass of wine again, that the world was a chaos to which my having or not having a glass of wine brought no greater sense of order.

The queen liked Montreal and had a close photographer friend, a Montrealer, with whom he was collaborating on a book of high-gloss photographs of drag performers. I met the friend there, even went on a road trip with her and two Parisians to Quebec City. We visited her grandmother—"*Grandmère Quebec!*" she told me to call her, in her rugged-sounding French—who sat with us late into the evening on the terrace of her suburban home, drinking and smoking. At one point she turned to me after I'd declined several offers of wine, beer, and cigarettes and said, "You don't drink, you don't smoke—what *do* you do?" I didn't know what to say. I was watching her, trying to understand what it meant to become a person, to grow old and gradually become one's irreversible self. I was twenty-five.

In Montreal I sublet a one-bedroom apartment in Laurier, on the French side of town. The tenant, a spritelike young blonde, left me her boyfriend's bicycle. I rode it all around the city (or "mill town," as an older gay friend and mentor had called it back in Berkeley, as in, "Why are you going to *that* mill town?") and often up and down the hills of Parc Mont-Royal, where I hoped to meet men. I was seriously off my game that summer, though—as evidenced, I guess, by the fact that, as an outgoing twenty-five-year-old who had been told ad nauseam that he was handsome and charming and so on and so forth, I eventually resorted to the bathhouse—and I never managed to connect with any guys. Not in parks, not in cafés, not in bars. I wanted so much to have a summer fling in Montreal. It was the closest thing to a summer fling in Paris I could afford.

I did meet an attractive young French-Canadian woman at the park one day. She was sitting with a friend when I pulled up on my bicycle to a neighboring bench. I'd intended to gaze upon nature, to project my erotic fantasies on it like a sexually frustrated bourgeois living in the nineteenth century and to read a bit of Sylvia Townsend Warner's *Kingdoms of Elfin*. As I settled in, the pair spoke to each other in French, glancing at me often.

"Excuse me," the young male friend called. "Are you single?" When the young woman, whom I'll call Marina, slapped his shoulder and apologized to me, I knew he had asked for her and not himself.

"Well, yes," I said, "but I'm gay."

A harassed look came over her. "Damn it!" she said. "Of course you're gay. Of course!" Marina was tall and slender. She held herself with easy confidence, perched in good posture on the bench, but had an air of mild exasperation, too, as though my gayness represented only the latest in a string of absurd injustices. She wore a dark blue sundress, a color that complemented her pale complexion and the long, black hair falling over her shoulders. Flattered to have a ravishing young woman notice and admire me, I apologized for being gay. The truth is that I wasn't the least bit sorry: being gay meant, if nothing else, theoretical protection against the possibility of physical intimacy between us—an intimacy that I felt might spring up, so to speak, in the natural course of things, which would in turn disorient me and expose my fractured humanity. I would've hated to have to face myself all over again, to reconsider myself, by wanting to sleep with a woman.

We got to talking, and though she lent her lament a comic air, there was a real ache behind her jokes about romantic frustration. "I can't meet a good man in Montreal to save my life," she said. "Everyone's gay and I'm going to die alone." I apologized for these things as well—first for being gay, then for her frustration, then for heterosexual men in general, who were all, we agreed, dogs. I knew her conundrum well: a state in which one's intense desire for a thing only makes it more elusive, mutating into a desperation that does no one any favors.

We exchanged phone numbers. I felt isolated in Montreal and was beginning to want to forget the drag queen, to forget that I'd longed to forget myself by forgetting myself all over again. The pleasure of a platonic and diverting summer friendship beckoned—a stopgap while I found another way to disappear, to chase sweet relief again.

So Marina and I met up now and then. She showed me another side of Montreal: she worked as an architect, and on strolls around town would point out noteworthy buildings. She took me to a favorite museum of hers where an exhibition of sculpture and ceramics was on. I don't remember any of the buildings or the art; I was too busy trying to be simultaneously present and unavailable. Because even though we were doing the gay friend–girlfriend thing, I couldn't deny a certain physical magnetism between us. This made our hanging out feel datelike at times, like inadvertent seduction, which gave rise to an all too human psychic distress. Uncomfortable silences would descend. I might look into her eyes with more intensity than I could help, feel too keenly the heat of standing close to her. What on earth, I wondered—afraid, probably, of the most obvious answer—what on earth were our bodies for?

Marina often circled back to her loneliness on these outings. "I don't understand," she would say. "I'm attractive, I'm intelligent, I'm an architect. I just don't get why I'm alone. I want to have a summer fling!" She would then look at me with more intensity, more hope than *she* could help. Eventually one of us would change the subject. I asked a lot of questions about architecture that summer, though I couldn't tell you today even one thing I learned about it.

It seems stupid to me now that I didn't surrender to instinct. We were both dancing around the idea, both lonesome and hard up, both drawn to each other. And from a distance of ten years it appears that the main thing holding me back was this protective conception of myself as a gay man and a gay man only—a *fundamentalist gay*, if you will. We could've just acknowledged the feeling and gone from there, maybe even talked the prospect into an early grave if it came to that, maybe shared a good laugh.

I remember an afternoon when a chance for us to fall into bed together came and went. We'd run into each other at a coffee shop in Mile End where I often went to read the news and write. Marina asked if I wanted to see her apartment, which wasn't far. I did, I said.

It was a one-bedroom, minimalist, clean—just how I'd imagine a young architect's apartment to be. Inside, we chatted in a casual way, her seated on her white, rumpled bed, me leaning against the door frame to her bedroom. The sun was shining through the windows; particles of dust floated in the light. There came a moment when we both fell silent, when I watched her from the threshold and she watched me back. Instinct stirred. I resisted. Why? Fear ruled my life too often. I wish I'd tried to face it, wrestle it to the ground, even just admit to it. "I'm a little frightened here," I might've said. Or I might have just, you know, done something, moved through it and into the new, the unknown.

What I said was this: "I'd better be going." I'd better disappear, dear. I turned after a too-long beat—one during which I hoped, I think, she might protest. That way I wouldn't have to and being human wouldn't be my fault.

———

Here are a few selling points taken from the websites of several Montreal bathhouses:

10,000 square feet of high sensations
it's up to you to get free of your clothing and take advantage of the
   pleasure of walking through an oasis *of real men*
Students always 50% off

To this I'll add: Sex without lasting connection is the hopeful center to which all hallways and blind turns lead. The lighting is extremely low, which not only flatters tired features but gives the place an air of fetishized sordidness, crime, imprisonment. Depending on your mood, this may seem thrilling, or banal, or like one of those homemade haunted-house affairs at Halloween— like something might jump out at the next pagan station, wailing, grabbing at you with a rubber hand. A far cry from how I imagined, as a teenager, winningly homoerotic Roman baths: august and marbled and clean, pure in the light of my Mediterranean fantasies. All our bathhouses, back rooms, dungeons, etc. inherit part of their atmosphere of Gothic decay by operating in the long shadow of AIDS. They are, in their way, ruins. Entering one—for someone like me, who was born around the time this plague began ravaging the gay community, who, again, was being raised on a small island near Seattle as this horror unfolded beyond his immediate sphere of awareness and so can only be said to have stepped out, as a young man, into the wreckage left behind—is like crossing into a realm where the shades of recent history roam, and not only because the majority of men there are often old enough to have lived through the annihilation by disease of so many of their friends and loved ones.

I wandered through the dark halls, puzzled by how empty the place seemed. I passed by a couple of muscular middle-aged men who clenched their jaws and bulged their eyes with the unmistakable intensity of addicts. Their come-ons were so crazed, so famished, that I couldn't bring myself to say yes. If only I'd been high, too. One, a tattooed, athletic dude with brown hair and wild eyes, squeezed his bulge when I saw him a second time, then whipped open the front of his towel. He said something I didn't understand, though I assumed it wasn't anything I might hear at a weekly French conversation group. Then he put his hand on my shoulder and gave me a pleading look.

"*Non, merci*," I said, pulling away. I put my hand up in the universal sign for "you're on too much meth." I sensed an aggressive turn coming. Sure enough, he started ranting at me, presumably taking issue with the fact that although I'd entered the bathhouse and had now been walking around for some time, I wasn't having sex with anyone. He brought a vial of poppers to one nostril—he'd been keeping it clenched in his fist—then held it toward me. I shook my head and began to walk away; this pissed him off even more, and in one swift motion he grabbed my neck and forced the vial under my nose. Enraged, I shoved him. The whiff of poppers left me unpleasantly lightheaded. I stood my ground, cursing him out in English while he berated me further in French. Finally, he retreated down the corridor.

Within moments another man appeared at the doorway of his private cell nearby, curious to see what the fuss was about. He looked friendly and reassuring—in his sixties, I guessed. I approached. He gave me a pat on the chest. "*Entrez*," he said, stepping aside.

He closed the door for privacy. We kissed for a couple minutes, caressed each other, sighed. The popper buzz faded. The man must have sensed my desire ebbing, too. "*Ça va?*" he said.

"*Un instant*," I said, pulling away. We both sat on the bench, side by side. A conversation followed in which I described having the bottle of poppers thrust beneath my nose by the tweaking muscle man and the fury I felt. It had rattled me more than I let my companion see—the high of the poppers, combined with the adrenal rush of fighting them off, left me trembling. My new acquaintance shook his head, saying, "*Non, non,*" adding that sex should be natural. "*Naturel, naturel!*" he insisted, by which he meant free of chemical influence, and though that wasn't my point, exactly, I half-agreed, saying, "Yes, something like that— something like natural." Maybe, he added, "*un petit peu de mari-juana,*" but he lamented all the meth, all the amyl nitrate, all the reliance on chemical highs.

I laughed a little. He rubbed my shoulder. There I sat in the cell of a man who'd no doubt come of age in the sixties, a quasi-Emersonian bathhouse hippie, a transparent gay eyeball who'd surely tasted his fair share of free love, seen no small amount of lesions, wasting, agony, disappearance. Sitting by him felt some-how safe, though as I told him that I wished we had *un petit peu de marijuana* right then, I wondered to myself: what was he still doing there, haunting this maze? What was I still doing there, foiled in my desire to escape from myself?

When I left, he told me to enjoy the rest of my *visite à Mon-tréal.* I made my way down the hall to my room. I closed the door and sat for many minutes on my own rented bench, rented towel wrapped around my waist. I dozed, unsure what to make of my life—my body, the freaked-out consciousness that inhabited it, the time I conceivably had left with that particular dynamic duo. What was it for? What an outrage that time was always going by, stealing things away: opportunities for pleasure, that much more of the life left in the body, every single piece of everything in the entire world and universe. That's right: I'd traveled many miles to be maudlin in a half-abandoned French-Canadian bath-house, to sit alone and speculate about what AIDS had wrought. And I hadn't even been drinking—I was still pretending to be a recovering drug addict and alcoholic. I never did know how to take a real vacation.

I changed back into my clothes, then stood in the middle of room 19, looking around. Somehow it felt like I'd forgotten something important, like I still had unfinished business in the bathhouse. But maybe it'll always feel like that, so long as history reaches forward, groping in the dark, grasping at us, forever unfinished, insatiable.

My summer fling with Montreal, such as it was, was ending. I couldn't wait to get back to California, made human again by my failure to find relief from being human. There I'd drift from the drag queen, my fantasies about sobriety and disappearance having passed like clouds across the open sky. I'd think of Marina now and then, but fall out of touch with her, too, aside from some stray messages traded through LinkedIn. Before I left the bathhouse, though, I had one more mistake to make.

Fully dressed, I returned to the antechamber with the low lighting and the chairs and the unmanned bar. No signs of life there: the attendant and friend no longer sat chatting. Wanting to show good manners, I had the odd thought that I should find the attendant and say good-bye—say *thank you*, of all things. I also wanted to be witnessed leaving. One feels a little less sure one *has* left, otherwise.

I paused before a latticed metal door that I assumed was an exit. The door had some signage in French on it, the meaning of which escaped me. Or maybe I spent too little time trying to puzzle it out. Or maybe I knew, somewhere in my heart, what would happen if I opened the door and wouldn't admit it to myself. Maybe I wanted to cause some trouble.

Whatever the case, the moment I pushed the door open, a

high, shrill alarm pierced the air. I froze, holding the door while this deafening sound filled not only the front room but the whole interior, the entire bathhouse.

The attendant stormed in then, a furious, horrified look on his face. He swatted toward me with his hand and shouted in French. I couldn't hear him over the alarm but started shouting back, "I'm sorry! I'm sorry!"

The hateful look on his face suggested that the alarm meant more than having to run to some control panel, flip a switch, shut the thing up—it seemed quite possible, in fact, that he didn't know *how* to turn it off. Though maybe that, too, was just another fantasy read into a face. Later I'd picture a handful of souls still moving within the maze, either lusting after some passing body or entangled already, suddenly startled apart, bringing their hands to their ears, their faces contorting in confusion. I'd imagine someone in the heart of the bathhouse letting his semen fly just as the alarm tripped. Someone else, dozing and sweating in the sauna, jolted awake as if from a frightful dream. I stepped out into the hallway, the latticed door slamming shut behind me. I couldn't help but look back at the scowling attendant, watch him disappear into the bowels of the bathhouse as though swallowed up by some powerful force. Some force other than my having introduced a major inconvenience into his workday, I mean. Later I'd imagine him making a full sweep of the labyrinth, checking every private cell, every scurvy corner, every shadow, the dry heat sauna, shouting to everyone over the alarm that they needed to get dressed and go, leave the bathhouse, some young fool, some *connard*, went out the wrong door.

It was years before I'd wonder why I ever thought anyone would have to leave. It was, after all, no longer a world of raids and roundups. Our sex was tolerated, in theory, to a greater extent than ever before, and soon there would be no reason to be alone, to be a ball-gagged slave in darkness, a confirmed bachelor, a strange man living by himself down the lane. Raid was just something we'd buy to kill insects. Roundup we'd buy to kill weeds. And while we pulled the dead weeds out, we'd tell each other stories about the things we'd done and seen on our trips to a vanishing world. "I went to Montreal once," I'd say, "in a past life. I was lonely in those days. So stupid with fear—so curious, too. I went into a bathhouse and I barely touched anyone. On my way out I set off the emergency exit alarm."

"How very fascinating," a friend, alive, would reply. "What happened after that?"

Acknowledgments

I would like to express my gratitude to the Virginia Center for the Creative Arts, the Lambda Literary Writers Retreat, Sozopol Seminars, and Arteles Creative Center for offering me time and space to work on these essays. Thanks are due, too, to the University of Iowa and to the La Hart-Van Bortels for their support.

My heartfelt thanks to Rakesh Satyal, whose fantastic editorial guidance helped to shape this collection into something larger than the sum of its parts. Thank you to Loan Le as well for all of her hard work and assistance, and to Stephanie Mendoza, publicist extraordinaire. It has been a delight to work with the whole team at Atria, who bring such great care, creativity, and humor to every step of the publishing process.

A huge thank-you to Jin Auh and Jessica Friedman of the Wylie Agency, who found great homes for many of these essays over the years and whose continual encouragement has meant the world to me.

Thank you to Lan Samantha Chang at the Iowa Writers' Workshop for her mentorship and for her inspiring example. Thank you also to Michelle Huneven, who read and encouraged many of these essays (and who edited one, "A Stranger in Siem Reap," for *The Los Angeles Review of Books*). And my other teachers at Iowa—Andrew Sean Greer, Allan Gurganus, James Alan MacPherson, and Wells Tower—to all of whom I am indebted for the many enlivening conversations about art and life that we shared. Thank you, of course and always, to the great Connie Brothers (happy retirement, Connie) and to Deb West and Jan Zenisek.

Many of these essays benefited from the advice of editors at the various publications in which they have appeared, and I would like to express my gratitude to them: to Ben Ryder Howe, Yuka Igarashi, Roger Hodge, Thessaly La Force, Jesse Ashlock, Sadie Stein, Philip Graham, and Mellissa Jessen-Hiser. Thank you to everyone at *The Iowa Review* and to Eula Biss for giving "Lovers' Theme" a home.

A special thank-you to Diana Cage, who taught the nonfiction workshop while I was at the Lambda Literary Retreat, and to everyone in our extraordinary cohort: Wendy Judith Cutler, Lourdes Follins, Chanelle Gallant, Dr. Jonathan Higgins, Tedd Kerr, Danny Thanh Nguyen, Rajat Singh, Aaron Tilford, Steffan Triplett, Tori Truscheit, and Ricky Tucker.

Another special thank-you to everyone I worked with at the Elizabeth Kostova Foundation's Sozopol Seminar on Creative Nonfiction: Elizabeth Kostova, Milena Deleva, Simona Ilieva, Philip Graham, Benjamin Moser. Thank you to my workshop mates Kate Angus, Akwaeke Emezi, Chris Fenton Thomas, and Jaclyn Moyer.

I thank the friends and readers who have helped me think through these works over the years and who have brought so much intelligence, passion, curiosity, and humor into my life: Emma Borges-Scott, Ellie Catton, Rachel Down, Angela Flournoy, Gerardo Herrera, Leslie Jamison, Carmen Maria Machado, Kannan Mahadevan, Kyle McCarthy, Ben Mauk, Andrew Nance, Yuly Restrepo, Rebecca Rukeyser, Bennett Sims, Hiya Swanhuyser, Steve Toussaint, and Tony Tulathimutte.

Thanks again to everyone at the bookstores where I worked while writing many of these pieces—to Jan Weismiller, Terry Cain, Kathleen Johnson, and Paul Ingram at Prairie Lights, and to the crew at Three Lives & Co.: Toby Cox, Troy Chatterton, Joyce McNamara, Carol Wald, Miriam Chotiner-Gardner, Ryan Murphy, Jo Stewart, Nora Shychuk, and Ruby Smith. Oh yeah, and thank you to Bob Bozic, whom I met at Three Lives and subsequently traveled with to Serbia and Bosnia—the trip of a lifetime.

Thank you to everyone at the Pierrepont School for your support and for the endlessly fascinating conversations across experiences and disciplines.

Love and gratitude to my family, who have always encouraged my writing and who have been wonderfully tolerant and philosophical when it comes to being written about. A special thank-you to my mother, whose sense of humor and whose example as an artist have always inspired me, and with whom I had many profound, enlightening conversations about the material in this book. Thank you to Tad and Tifani, to Mary and Mike and Jim, and to the darling, delightful little ones: Mariko, Ryota, Koji, and Ren.

Last, thank you, Hilton, for your love and support, for your beautiful spirit, and for all the life and laughter we continue to share.

About the Author

Evan James was born in Seattle. He is the author of the novel *Cheer Up, Mr. Widdicombe*. His work has appeared in *Travel + Leisure, Oxford American, The New York Times*, and other publications. He is a graduate of the Iowa Writers' Workshop and has received fellowships from Yaddo, Virginia Center for the Creative Arts, and the Lambda Literary Writers' Retreat, where he was an Emerging LGBTQ Voices Fellow. He lives in New York.

SONOMA
COUNTY
LIBRARY

to renew • para renovar

707.566.0281

sonomalibrary.org